Mastering the Basics of Technical English

과학기술 영작문의 기본

Richard Cowell · 佘 錦華 共著

이재호 譯

탐구당

머 리 말

국제교류 증가와 기업의 해외진출과 더불어 기술영어(技術英語 Technical English) 작문 능력은 연구자 · 기술자에겐 필요불가결한 것이 되었다. 이러한 필요에 응하기 위해 기술영어 쓰기에 관한 책들이 출판되고 있다. 대부분의 책들은 틀린 문장들(incorrect sentences)의 예를 구체적으로 보여주고, 올바른 영어(Correct English)로 고치는 형식으로 구성되어 있다.

이런 책들과는 달리 이 책에서는 영작문을 할 적에 자주 잘못 사용하는 단어들(words)과 표현(expressions)을 지적하여 오류(mistake)의 이유를 깨닫게 할 뿐만 아니라, 동시에 한국식 발상(發想)에서 벗어난, 한층 더 자연스러운 영어쓰기의 안내자 역할을 하는 것이 매우 중요하다고 우리는 생각한다. 그런데 이런 관점에서 쓰인 책은 거의 눈에 띄지 않는다. 이러한 상황을 참작하여, 필자들은 이 새로운 관점에서 기술영어(Technical English) 쓰기에 관한 책을 내기로 결심하였다.

이 책에서는 한국인 연구자들이 자주 잘못 쓰고 있는 표현들의 쓰임새에 대해 가이드라인(제시)과, 문체(style)와 구두법(句讀法)에 관한 기본적 힌트를 제공한다. 가이드라인들 만을 제공하기 때문에, 모든 것을 망라하고 있지는 않다. 즉 이 책의 가이드라인을 따른다면, 독자는 올바른 영어 문장을 쓸 수 있을 것이다. 영어가 모국어인 사람들이 쓴 문장 중에 독자는 이 책의 가이드라인을 따르지 않은 문장들과 마주칠 수도 있을 것이다. 또 지금까지의 책들과는 달리, 이 책은 독자들로 하여금 자기의 이해도(理解度 level of understanding)를 확인할 수 있도록, 중요한 항목 뒤에, 연습문제도 제공했다. 이 책을 활용하기 위해서는 독자들은 상세한 영문법 지식이 필요 없고, 기본적인 문법만 알고 있으면 충분하다. 단어와 표현들은 의미(意味 meaning)와 사용법(使用法 usage)이란 두 주요한 측면을 갖고 있지만, 많은 사람들은 영한사전에서 단어의 의미를 찾아보는 것만으로, 그 단어를 영어문장에서 자유롭게 사용할 수 있다고 여기는 경향이 흔히 있는듯 하다. 그러나 단어의 의미를 안다는 것은 그 단어를 읽는 능력을 준다는 것 일뿐, 그 단어로 문장을 쓰려고 하면, 많은 잘못(mistake)을 저지르게 된다. 즉 그 단어를 써서 문장을 작

성하려고 하면, 독자는 자연히 한국어식 영문(英文)을 쓰게 된다. 올바른 문장을 쓰기 위해서는 그 단어의 사용법(usage)을 마스터할 필요가 있다. 이 책에는 올바른 사용법(correct usage)에 관한 길라잡이로 가득 차 있다. 저자들은, 20년 이상 영문기술논문을 첨삭(添削)하는 동안에, 똑같은 잘못이 되풀이 되는 것을 깨달았다. 그 경험에 바탕을 두고서 이 책의 토픽을 선택하고 맨 처음에서 끝까지 가장 틀리기 쉬운 단어, 표현들 순서대로 배열하였다.

이 책에 사용된 예문들은, 주로 정보 · 전자분야의 것이지만, 이 분야에 낯선 독자라도, 전문용어(Technical Terms)를 단순한 단어로 바꿔 채우고, 사용법 패턴(usage pattern)에 주목한다면, 이 책에서 많은 혜택을 얻으리라고 확신한다. 예컨대 section 1의 [apply]에, 아래와 같은 전형적인 잘못과 그 첨삭을 보여준다.

× *Many attempts have been made to apply the microphase-separated domains of block copolymer as a dry-etching mask.*

○ Many attempts have been made to **use** the microphase-separated domains of block copolymer **as** a dry-etching mask.

– 위의 문장의 패턴을 꺼내어 보면

× *...to apply(a substance) as (something)*

○ ...to **use** (a substance) **as** (something)

저자들은 독자들이 기술영어 작문에 이 책이 쓸모 있다고 여긴다면 몹시 만족스러워 할 것이다.

2006년 4월

리처드 카우얼 · 진후아 셰

Preface

With the increasing interchange among nations and the advance of businesses into foreign countries, the ability to write technical English has become indispensable to researchers and engineers. To meet this need, many books have been published on how to write technical English. Most of them take the form of showing concrete examples of incorrect sentences and then the correct English. In contrast, we think it is also very important to consider words and expressions that readers may often misuse, and not only help to understand the reason for the mistake and the correct usage, but at the same time provide guidance in writing more natural English that gets away form the Korean way of thinking, However, it is almost impossible to find any books written from this point of view. In light of this situation, the authors decided to put out a book on writing technical English from this new viewpoint.

This book provides guidelines on the usage of words and expressions that are often misused by Korean researchers, and some basic tips on style and punctuation. Since it contains only guidelines, it is not an exhaustive study. That is, if you follow the guidelines, your sentences will be correct; but in articles written by native speakers of English, you may come across sentences that do not follow the suggestions in this book. Furthermore, unlike other books, this one contains exercises after many of the topics to enable readers to check their level of understanding. To use the book, readers do not need a detailed knowledge of English grammar; a familiarity with basic grammar will suffice.

Two key aspects of any word or expression are **meaning** and **usage**. It seems that there is a common tendency for people to look up the meaning of a

Preface

word in an English-Korean dictionary, and then to feel that they can use the word freely in an English sentence. This is the cause of many mistakes, because knowing the meaning of a word just gives you the ability to **read** it. In other words, when you try to write a sentence with it, you naturally follow the Korean usage. In order to **write** correctly, you must also know the **usage**. This book is filled with guidance on correct usage.

The topics covered in this book are the result of over 20 years of experience correcting technical papers written in English by Japanese researchers, and the realization that the same mistakes keep appearing again and again. The book is loosely organized with the most common problems at the beginning and less frequently occurring problems at the end.

Almost all of the example sentences come from the fields of electronics and information technology. However, readers not familiar with these fields can still obtain great benefit from this book by substituting simple words for the very technical terms and focusing on usage patterns. For example, the following sentences from the topic "apply" in Section 1 illustrate a typical mistake and how to correct it:

× *Many attempts have been made to <u>apply</u> the microphase-separated domains of block copolymer <u>as</u> a dry-etching mask.*

○ Many attempts have been made to **use** the microphase-separated domains of block copolymer **as** a dry-etching mask.

Extracting the pattern from the sentence, we obtain the following.

× *...to apply(a substance) as (something)*

○ ...to **use** (a substance) **as** (something)

In fact, all readers should focus on usage patterns so that they can apply them to their own writing.

The authors would be very pleased if the readers found this book at all useful in their writing of technical English.

April, 2006

Richard Cowell & Jin-Hua She

Contents

Section 1

realize

confirm

adopt

evaluate vs. estimate

first vs. at first

propose

apply

Punctuation : Space

Style : Dynamic Verbs 1

Prepositions 1

realize

[실현하다]라는 말을 영역하는 경우, 상황에 따라 여러 가지로 번역하는 방법이 있다. 단지 기계적으로 [realize]라고 번역하는 걸로는 대부분의 경우 틀렸음에 주의하자.

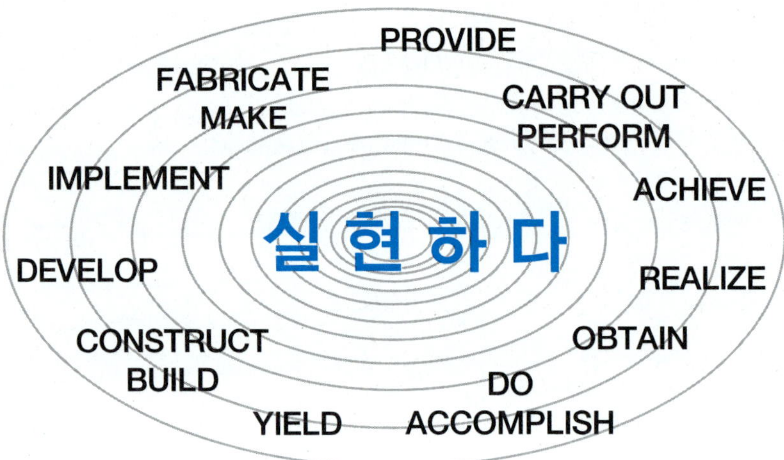

DEFINITION:

1. **디자인** 또는 **아이디어**를 realize한다는 것은, 물리적인 형태로 만드는 것이다. 그림을 그리거나 기계를 제작하는 것이 그 예이다.
2. **기대**, **욕구**, **대망(大望)**, **꿈**, **이상(理想)** 등을 realize한다는 것은 그것을 실현하는 것이다.

realize + 가상(假想)적인것 · 상상(想像)적인 것

Realize vs. 실현하다

한국어로 :
구체적인 것을 실현할 수 있다.

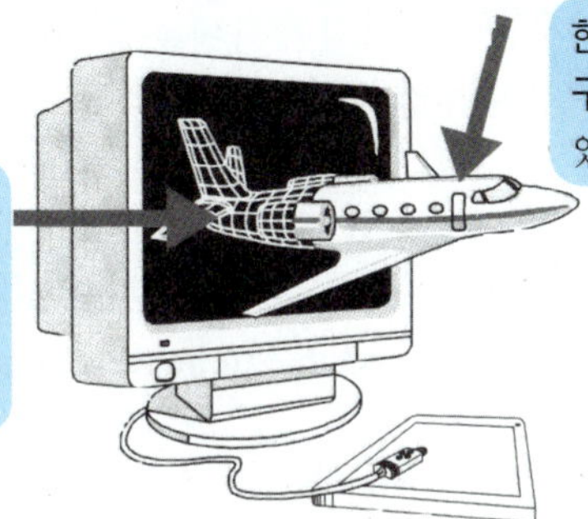

영어로 :
Realize 되는 것은 구체적인 것이 아니라, **디자인**이든가 **아이디어**이다.

한국어로는 [실현하다]를, 흔히 특정한 목표 · 목적을 실현한(하는) 경우 또는 일을 완성한 경우에 쓰인다. 영어에서는 [realize]는 주로 장래의 일 및 아이디어 또는 개념(槪念)의 실현가능성에 주목하고 있기 때문에 특정한 연구목표 · 목적에는 쓰지 않는다. 또 과거형[realized]는 기술영어(技術英語)에는 거의 쓰지 않는다.

[Realize]를 쓰는 경우는 매우 적다.

GOOD EXAMPLES

○ If such a system **is ever realized**, it will have many advantages.
  • 그런 시스템은 실제로 존재하지 않고, 아이디어뿐이다.

○ To **realize** ultrafast optical communications, we need...
  • 그런 통신수법(通信手法)은 현재의 시점에서 실제론 존재하지 않는다.

○ There are several bottlenecks that have so far prevented **realization of the full potential** of this type of system.

○ If these ideas are **realizable**, they should help a great deal by...

○ If devices meeting all these requirements are **realizable**, they can be used in many applications.

○ These results show that multigigahertz RF circuits with inductors are **realizable** on SOI wafers with digital circuits.

[realize] 대신에

다음 동사를 써서 그 사용법(각각의 동사에 어울리는 목적어)을 마스터하면, 작문(作文)은 한층 더 정확해지며 알기 쉽게 된다.

[동사 : 회색　목적어 : 칼라색]

achieve	goal, target (목표, 목적)

- This circuit scheme makes it possible to **achieve high speed and low power** at a supply voltage of 0.5 V.
- These networks require smaller, cheaper modulator modules with a lower loss and a larger number of channels. **To achieve these** goals, we developed ...
- A dielectric filter was employed to **achieve good** absolute-wavelength **control**.
- **To achieve an ultrahigh** f_t, it is essential that the base layer be thinner.

build construct make	system, network, link, module, package, component, equipment, facility, etc. (시스템, 네트워크, 링크, 모듈, 패키지, 콤포넌트, 설비, 시설 등)

- ... to **build/construct/make** more cost-effective **packages**
- ... to **build/construct/make** high-performance **equipment**
- ... to **build/construct** practical terabit-class transmission **systems**

carry out perform	procedure, process, operation, experiment, test, measurement, analysis, simulation, modeling, calculation, research, study, work, etc (수순(手順), 프로세스, 오퍼레이션, 실현, 테스트, 계측(計測), 분석, 시뮬레이션, 모델링, 계산, 조사, 연구, 일 등)

- ... to **carry out/perform** a retiming **operation**
- ... to **carry out/perform** a numerical **analysis**
- ... to **carry out/perform** bias-temperature stress **tests**
- ... to **carry out/perform** high-temperature **annealing**

fabricate make	device, circuit, structure, etc. (디바이스, 회로(回路), 구조 등)

- ... to **fabricate** ultrahigh-speed **ICs**

- ... to **fabricate** a low-loss single-mode photonic-crystal **waveguide**
- ... to **fabricate** a 1-V band-pass **filter**
- ... to **fabricate** a MEMS **structure**

implement	function, scheme, logic, etc. (기능, 스킴, 로직 등)

- ... to **implement** a pseudo-differential **scheme**
- ... to **implement** a regeneration **function**
- ... to **implement** CAM control **logic**
- ... to **implement** an optical Fourier **transform**

obtain	result, value, characteristic, etc. (결과, 수치, 특성 등)

- We **obtained** a power penalty of less than 1 dB.
- Tensile-strained bulk InGaAsP was used to **obtain** polarization insensitivity.
- Error-free operation **was obtained** on all channels.
- These curves of output power versus photocurrent **were obtained** by feeding an optical pulse train into the photodiode.

provide	desired characteristic, information, service, etc. (바라는 특성, 정보, 서비스 등)

- Portable electronic devices **provide** advanced mobile digital **services**.
- These MQW layers **provide** excellent extinction **characteristics**.
- This type of package **provides** a large number of **inputs and outputs**.
- the batteries **provide** a **backup time** of 3 hours.

yield	[To yield means to produce as a result.] (「결과로서 낳다」 경우에 쓰인다.)

- Using the conventional method does not always **yield** accurate results.
- Focusing light within a very narrow space should **yield** very efficient second-harmonic generation.
- Even a 10-dBm laser can **yield** a power density of 100 MW/cm^2.
- Optimization of the fabrication conditions should **yield** a higher efficiency.
- The data "10110100" were successfully inverted to **yield** "01001011".

PRACTICE

[실현하다]의 영어번역은 [realize]대신, 다음과 같은 말들이 쓰인다.

accomplish/do	fabricate/make	obtain
achieve	perform/carry out	provide
build/construct	implement	yield

위의 선택지(選擇肢)에서 적당한 말을 모두 선택하여 다음 구(句)를 완성하라.

1. ____________________ a device
2. ____________________ a large bandwidth
3. ____________________ a function
4. ____________________ a component
5. ____________________ a digital/analog converter(circuit)
6. ____________________ oxidation
7. ____________________ basic operations
8. ____________________ a large bandwidth-efficiency product [product=積]
9. ____________________ a system
10. ____________________ an IC
11. ____________________ control
12. ____________________ wavelength conversion
13. ____________________ an exclusive-or gate(circuit)
14. ____________________ accurate results
15. ____________________ a numerical analysis

confirm

POINT

영어의 [confirm]과 비교하면, 한국어의 [확인한다]쪽의 의미가 넓다. [확인한다]를 쉽사리 [confirm]이라고 번역해서는 안 된다.

다음 표현을 보자.

- 무엇이 일어났는가를 **확인한다** to **ascertain/find out/determine** what happened 이 경우 [확인한다]를 [confirm]으로 번역해서는 안 된다.
  아래는 「confirm」의 매우 흔히 쓰는 예이다.
- 호텔 예약을 **확인하다. confirm** a hotel reservation

호텔 예약을 확인하려면, 미리 예약되어 있어야 한다. 즉, 두 단계가 된다. : (1) **먼저** 호텔을 예약하고, (2) **그 후**, 그 예약을 확인한다. 기술영어(技術英語)에서 [confirm]을 쓰기위해선 꼭 같이 첫 단계가 필요하다.

DEFINITION: 가설(假說) 또는 기술(記述)의 올바름을 무엇인가로 confirm 한다는 것은 그 가설 또는 기술이 확실히 틀림없음을 **입증하는** 것이다.

NOTE [Confirm]을 쓰는데는, 다음 **두 요소**가 필요하다.

1. 무엇인가가 옳다는 **이전(以前)의 생각(말했던 것).**
2. 그 생각(말했던 것)이 옳다는 것을 입증하는 **새로운 확증**. 이 확증에 의해 앞의 생각(말했던 것)은 입증된다.

1. First statement	2. Confirmation
According to my theory, a ray of light passing near the Sun is bent slightly in the direction of the Sun' s mass (내 이론에 따르면, 태양 근처를 통과하는 광선은 태양쪽으로 약간 휘어진다.)  	Our observations confirm Einstein' s prediction! (우리들의 관측결과는 아인슈타인의 예언을 입증했다.) 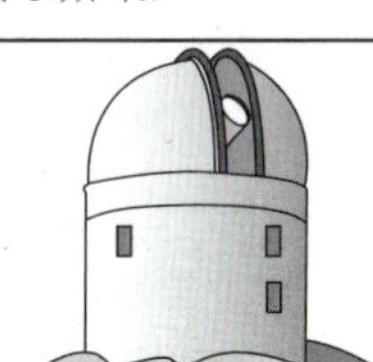

GOOD EXAMPLES

- Sato et al.presented the **first experimental evidence** of phosphorus pile-up at the Si/Sio2interface. ... **Their discovery was confirmed** by sheet resistance measurements and neutron activation analysis.
- When the effect of the extended current path becomes greater than that of the straight path, the series resistance **should have** a rather pronounced effect. **To confirm this supposition**, we fabricated circular devices with a higher ratio of gate area to emitter area.
- One milestone in our development effort is the use of our ICs in fully electrical TDM transmission experiments at 40 Gbit/s, which fully **confirmed our belief** that such systems are not only feasible, but also well within our reach.
- We **confirmed the validity of these approximations** by comparing them with the results of a numerical analysis.
- These results **confirm** that the system performs **as designed**.

다만 실험결과를 말하는 경우 [confirm]을 쓰지 않도록 하라.

TYPICAL MISTAKES

demonstrate

× *These results confirm that the device outputs a signal from the proper port.*

- 이 문장을 단지 실험 결과의 의미를 설명하고 있다. 이 결과는 앞서 말했던 것의 올바름을 입증하는 새로운 확증은 아니다.

○ These results **demonstrate** that the device outputs a signal from the proper port.

× *We confirmed that these techniques will be very useful in developing high-speed, high-density packages.*

○ We **demonstrated** that these techniques will be very useful in developing high-speed, high-density packages.

determine

× *We measured the change in weight of the electrodes to confirm whether or not deposition occurred.*

○ We measured the change in weight of the electrodes **to determine whether or not** deposition occurred.

~~Confirm~~  **assess/evaluate**

× *A test was performed in order to confirm the effectiveness of the method.*

○ A test was performed in order to **assess/evaluate** the effectiveness of the method.

× *The following experiments were performed to confirm this model.*

○ The following experiments were performed to **assess/evaluate** the validity of this model.

~~Confirm~~  **obtain**

× *Error-free operation of the device was confirmed.*

○ Error-free operation of the device **was obtained**.

~~Confirm~~  **demonstrate**

× *A test chip was fabricated to confirm error-free operation of the circuit.*

○ A test chip was fabricated to **verify** error-free operation of the circuit.

× *To confirm that wavelength conversion was efficient, we conducted another experiment.*

○ To **verify** that wavelength conversion was efficient, we conducted another experiment.

~~Confirm~~  **ensure**

× *We conducted field tests to confirm that the system worked properly in a regular service configuration.*

○ We conducted field tests to **ensure** that the system worked properly in a regular service configuration.

adopt

DEFINITION: 어떤 행동의 책략(策略), 계획, 방법, 방침(方針) 등을 adopt 한다는 것은, 그것을 선택하거나 또는 사용하기로 하고 실제로 사용하기 시작하는 것이다.

POINT

어느 방법을 선택할 것인가?

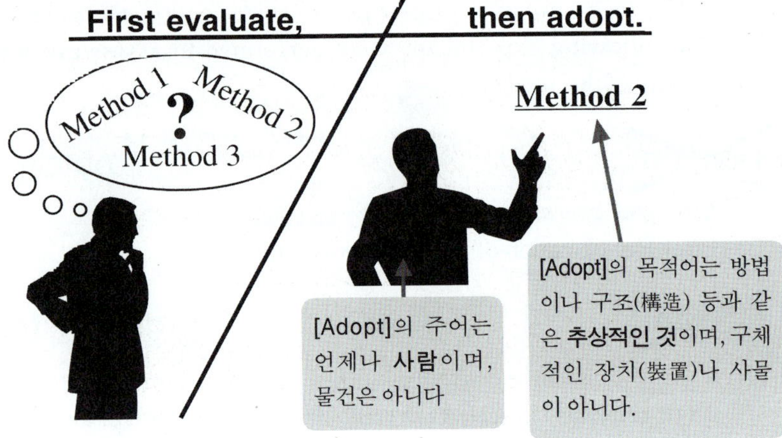

기술영어에서는 [adopt]를 쓰는 장면은 적다.

GOOD EXAMPLES

- To achieve these goals, we **adopted** a new **architecture**.
- The Standards Committee **adopted** our **framework**.
- One solution is to **adopt** a mixed **design**.
- So, we have abandoned Microsoft Windows and have instead **adopted** **LINUX**.

실제로 한 일을 설명하는 경우

실제로 한 일(실험, 계산, 제작(製作), 설계(設計) 등)을 설명할 때 [use] 또는 [employ]를 쓴다.

use, employ

method 2 was used to ...

Device A was employed to...

TYPICAL MISTAKES

× *These machines generally adopt superconducting bending magnets.*

- [Adopt]의 주어는 인간이어야 한다.

○ These machines generally **employ** superconducting bending magnets.

× *This illustrates the design method we adopted.*

- 무엇을 했는지를 설명할 뿐이며, [adopt]는 이렇게 쓰지 않는다.

○ This illustrates the design method we **used**.

× *We adopted this type of transistor because...*

- 물리적 장치(裝置)는 [adopt] 할 수 없다.

○ We **employed/selected** this type of transistor because...

× *To obtain high speed, we adopted a gate width ratio of 0.5.*

- 수치(數值)는 [adopt] 할 수 없다.

○ ... we **used** a gate width ratio of 0.5.

○ ... we **set** the gate width ratio **to** 0.5.

× *This amplifier adopts a successive-detection architecture.*

- [Adopt]의 주어는 인간이어야 한다.

○ This amplifier **employs/is based on** a successive-detection architecture.

evaluate vs. estimate

POINT

[평가하다]의 영어는 여러 가지 있다. 단 기계적으로[evaluate] 라고 번역하면, 틀릴 가능성이 높다.

DETERMINE
IDENTIFY
ASSESS
EXAMINE
MEASURE **평가하다** INVESTIGATE

good/bad EVALUATE suitable/unsuitable

ESTIMATE 0.02 μm 451℃ 38.453

DEFINITION: 무엇인가를 evaluate 한다는 것은, 좋은 점과 나쁜 점을 검토하며 그 중요성, 가치, 또는 질(質)을 결정하는 것이다.

NOTE Evaluate의 결과는 좋은가 나쁜가, 적절한가 부적절한가, 적당한가 적당하지 않은가, 충분한가 불충분한가이며, **수량(數量)이 아니다.**

~~evaluate~~  Good/Bad

○ We fabricated a test device in order to **evaluate its performance**.

○ We **evaluated the effectiveness** of our new method.

DEFINITION: 수량(數量)을 estimate 한다는 것은, 대충 **계산(計算) · 계측(計測)을 한**다는 것이다.

NOTE Estimate의 결과는 수량(數量)이다.

~~estimate~~  12.789

○ We **estimated the length** to be about 0.2 μm.

○ We can **estimate the capacitance** from the period of the voltage oscillations.

TYPICAL MISTAKES

× *We <u>evaluated the change</u> in the refractive index.*

○ We **estimated the change** in the refractive index.

× *The controller <u>evaluates</u> the matching <u>ratio</u> from the comparison results for each pixel.*

○ The controller **calculates** the matching **ratio** from the comparison results for each pixel.

× *This is a simple method of <u>evaluating the height</u> of a silicon structure.*

○ This is a simple method of **determining/estimating the height** of a silicon structure.

× *Next, we <u>evaluated the electrical characteristics</u> at room temperature.*

○ Next, we **measured the electrical characteristics** at room temperature.

× *This procedure was used to <u>evaluate</u> the dependence of phase shift on bias level.*

○ This procedure was used to **examine/determine** the dependence of phase shift on bias level.

PRACTICE

PART A : [Evaluate]나 [estimate] 또는 둘다를 써서 다음 빈칸을 매워라.

1. ________________________ the crystal quality
2. ________________________ the defect density
3. ________________________ the width
4. ________________________ the switching time
5. ________________________ the performance of the device
6. ________________________ the method
7. ________________________ the usefulness of the technique

8. ______________________ the difference in length

9. ______________________ the size of the fluctuations

10. ______________________ the efficiency of the process

11. ______________________ the time required

PART B : 다음 문장에 [evaluate]를 사용하는 것은 적절치 않다. [Evaluate] 대신 아래의 선택지(選擇肢)에서 적절한 단어를 골라 빈칸을 매워라.

determine	estimate	examine	identify
investigate	measure	observe	

1. The depth of the holes was ______________________ from microscope images.
2. The contaminants(오염물질 汚染物質) were ______________________ by thermal desorption spectroscopy.
3. The structure was ________________ with a microscope.
4. To ______________________ the effect of applying a voltage, we measured the composition of the surface.
5. The uniformity of the patterns was ______________________ by measuring the intensity of diffracted light.
6. Atomic force microscopy is now widely used to ______________________ surface structures.
7. We ______________________ the dependence of current of voltage.

first vs. at first

POINT

[At first]는 잘못해서 [first]란 의미로 쓰이는 일이 많다.

[First]는 다음 두 가지 용도(用途) 밖에 없다.

일련(一連)의 행동의 순번(順番)	리스트의 항목(項目)
First	First
Next	Second
Then	Third
After that	Fourth
Finally	Last

GOOD EXAMPLES

- Figure 3 illustrates the fabrication process. **First**, Cu interconnection patterns are formed... **Next**, a very thin Al film is deposited. Then, annealing is carried out... **After that**, the Al on the SiO_2 is selectively removed... Finally, the sample is heated to 350℃ ...

- This paper **first** explains the current modulation mechanism. **Next**, some experimental results are presented to show that...

- Oxygen species affect the composition through various kinetic routes. **First**, oxygen atoms coming from... **Second**, oxygen atoms can be directly incorporated...**Third**, activated oxygen species react...

- However, this configuration posed certain problems. **The first** is the requirement for a more compact system. **The second** problem is the need to prevent dust and eye injuries. **The third** issue is producibility.

- This study had two purposes. **The first** was to clarify the mechanism... **The second** was to estimate the lifetime...

[At first]는 변화(變化)하는 상황(狀況)을 묘사하는 데 쓰인다.

○ **At first**, it was sunny; **but later**, it got cloudy.

기술영어에서는 [at first]를 거의 쓸 필요가 없다.

GOOD EXAMPLES

○ We start with a gate voltage of zero, and then increase it. **At first**, there are no excess electrons in the island. **But** when the gate voltage crosses the dotted line, one electron tunnels through into the island.

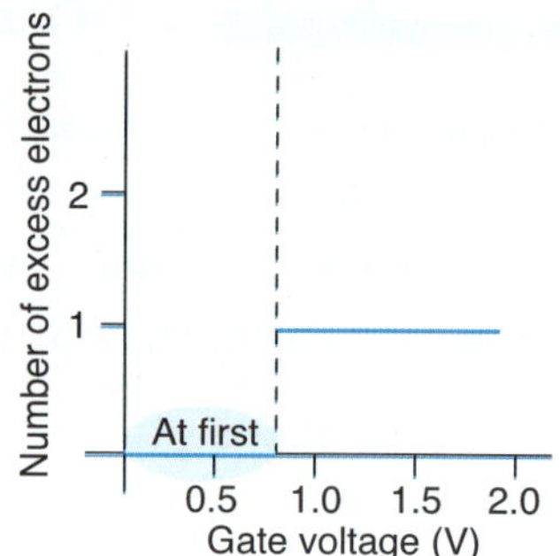

○ This figure illustrates how cooling affects the stress in a film. The stress does not increase very much **at first** because the generation of dislocations relieves it. **But** below 400℃, it rises rapidly.

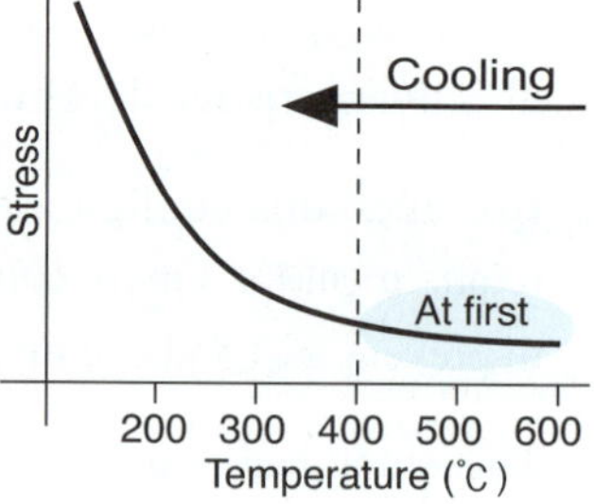

propose

POINT

기본적으로 [propose]라는 단어는 과학계(科學界)에 새로운 발상(發想)을 제안하는데 쓰인다. 단지 새로운 것을 나타내거나, 또는 새로운 것을 제작(製作)한 것을 보고하는 경우에는, [propose]는 쓰이지 않는다.

DEFINITION: 계획, 아이디어, 수법(手法) 등을 propose 한다는 것은, 다른 사람이 검토(그래서 대개 사용), 또는 판단 할 수 있도록 그것을 제안하는 것이다.

NOTE 예를 들면, 새로운 표준을 표준화위원회에 propose 하는 경우, 표준화위원회는 그것을 채택할 것인가 아닌가를 결정 짓는다. 또 다른 연구자가 자유롭게 사용할 수 있는 새로운 기술을 제안하는 경우, [propose]를 써도 좋다. 더욱이 새로운 이론적 개념을 제안하고, 그것을 다른 연구자한테 테스트 · 검증받고 싶은 경우에도 [propose]를 써도 좋다.

GOOD EXAMPLES

- ○ H.A. Lorentz **proposed** <u>the electron theory</u> of electrical charge in 1895; and in 1897, J.J. Thomson of England showed that the Edison effect current was indeed caused by negatively charged particles(electrons).
- ○ Peng and Tamir [10] first **proposed** <u>the use of blazed grating couplers</u>.
- ○ In this paper, we **propose** <u>a new concept</u> for ultrafast digital ICs made with traveling-wave FETs called traveling-wave FET logic.
- ○ The mean opinion score for harmonic vector excitation coding(HVXC) was the best among all <u>the</u> **proposed** <u>coders</u>. After core experiments were carried out as part of the standardization process, HVXC was chosen to be the ISO/IEC International Standard for MPEG-4 Audio.
  - MPEG-4 오디오 표준의 후보(候補)로서 코더가 제안(提案) 되어, 표준화 위원회가 어느것이 제일 좋은가를 결정했다.

[Propose]를 쓰는 장면(場面)은 적다.

1. 문제를 해결하거나 또는 목표를 달성하기 위하여, 새로운 것을 develop 한다 또는 devise 한다는 표현을 쓰기로 하자. 단지 새로운 것을 제작(製作)한 사실(事實)을 보고하는 경우엔 [propose]를 쓰지 말자.

~~propose~~  **develop, devise**

× *Coupling to a fiber is a serious problem with Si wire waveguides. To solve it, we* *<u>proposed</u>* *a spot-size converter.*

- 디바이스를 propose 한다는 것은, 그 개념을 보여주고 올바르게 가동(稼動)하는 것을 주장하는 것이다. 이 경우 디바이스는 또 아이디어의 단계(段階)로, **현실화 되어 있지 않다**는 함의(含意 implication)가 강하다. 만일, 이미 제작된 실험적 검증도 한 것이라면, [propose]를 쓰는 것을 잘못이다.

○ Coupling to a fiber is a serious problem with Si wire waveguides. To solve it, we **developed/devised** a spot-size converter.

× *We* *<u>proposed</u>* *a new circuit configuration to achieve high speed.*

○ We **developed/devised** a new circuit configuration to achieve high speed.

× *We* *<u>have proposed</u>* *what we call a chip-size cavity package that...*

○ We **have developed/devised** what we call a chip-size cavity package that...

2. 새로운 디바이스, 수법(手法)등에 [the proposed X] 라고 하지 말것. 특히 앞서 설명했듯이, [proposed device]란 실재(實在) 하지 않는 것이라는데 주의하라.

~~propose~~  **(Nothing), new, fabricated**

× *This graph shows the power dissipation of the* *<u>proposed</u>* *circuit.*

- 제안하는 회로(回路)는 아직 현실화 되어 있지 않기 때문에, 파워의 소산(消散)은 계측(計測) 되어 있지 않다.

○ This graph shows the power dissipation of **the** circuit. (... **our new** circuit, ...a **fabricated** circuit.)

× *For the <u>proposed</u> etching process, the etching rate was 389 nm/min.*

○ For the **new** etching process, the etching rate was 389 nm/min.

× *The <u>proposed</u> interconnection provides a low connection loss.*

○ **This** interconnection provides a low connection loss. (**The new** interconnection...)

× *The reflectivity obtained by the <u>proposed</u> method converges rapidly to the target value.*

○ The reflectivity obtained by **this** method converges rapidly to the target value. (...by our new method...)

3. 아래의 왼쪽의 연구에 관한 명사(동사)와 오른쪽의 발표에 관한 동사(명사)를 함께 사용하는 것은 흔히 바람직 하지 않다. 특히 [study]는 [propose]와 관계없음에 주의하라.

연구실에서 하는 것:		연구결과를 발표하는 방법:
study research work etc.	명사	paper report presentation etc.
그 목적:		그 목적:
develop devise invent create etc.	동사	report on describe present (propose) etc.

× *In this <u>study</u>, we <u>propose</u> a circuit technique to suppress...*

○ In this **study**, we **developed/devised** a circuit technique to suppress...

× *The purpose of this <u>study</u> was to <u>propose</u> an algorithm for...*

○ The purpose of this **study** was to **devise/develop** an algorithm for...

논문 또는 프리젠테이션의 목적은, 흔히 새로운 것을 보고 · 설명 · 소개하는 일이며, 그것을 propose 하는 것이 아니다.

  report, describe, present

× *In this paper, we <u>propose</u> a fabrication technique that can prevent...*

- 기술논문집(技術論文集)에 수록되어 있는 많은 논문은 논리적 또는 실험적 연구 결과를 보고하는 것이며, 무언가를 propose 하는 것이 아니다.

○ This paper **reports on/describes/presents** a fabrication technique that can prevent...

× *In this presentation, I'll <u>propose</u> a new micromechanical switch.*

○ In this presentation, I'll **describe** a new micromechanical switch.

× *Recently, we <u>proposed</u> a new multiple QPM structure...*

○ Recently, We **reported on** a new multiple QPM structure...

× *Various verification algorithm <u>have been proposed.</u>*

○ Various verification algorithm **have been reported**.

PRACTICE

아래 문장에서는 [PROPOSE] 또는 [PROPOSED]가 삭제되어 있다. 대신에 가장 적절한 단어를 골라 빈칸을 채워라.

1. To solve the problem, we ______________ a new circuit.
2. This shows the structure of ______________ transistor.
3. To provide sufficient flexibility and good performance, we ______________ new hardware and software architectures.
4. This paper ______________ a dynamic flip-flop circuit with a low power consumption.
5. By extending the principle of a temperature-insensitive optical filter, we ______________ a new temperature-insensitive arrayed-waveguide grating.
6. Recently, various methods of reducing the dislocation density have been ______________, such as epitaxial lateral overgrowth and pendeo-epitaxy.

apply

POINT

다음 페이지에 나와있는 [그 밖의 사용법]이외에는, [apply]의 목적어는 디바이스, IC, 설비(設備)등과 같은 구체적인 것(유형물 有形物)이 아니다.

DEFINITION: 일 또는 활동에 아이디어, 프로세스, 수법(手法) 등을 apply 한다는 것은, 그것을 일 또는 활동에 맞추어 사용하는 것이다.

APPLY + 추상적인 것 + to + 활동

GOOD EXAMPLES

apply idea to fabrication

○ To **apply** this idea **to** the fabrication of transistors, we need to use a low growth temperature...

apply lithography to production

○ In order to apply X-ray lithography **to** the mass production of future generations of electronic devices, high-performance exposure characteristics are required.

apply techniques to design

○ This section explains how to **apply** the techniques described above **to** the design of baseband circuits.

apply technique to assembly

○ This packaging technique **has been applied to** the assembly of all-optical wavelength converter module.

구체적인 사물을 apply 한다고는 말하지 않는다.

~~apply + 구체적인 사물~~  use

TYPICAL MISTAKES

× *This amplifier can be applied to single-conversion transceivers.*

- 유형물(有形物)을 apply 할 수가 없다.

○ This amplifier **can be used in** single-conversion transceivers.

× *This transistor <u>can be applied to</u> high-speed digital ICs.*
○ This transistor **can be used to make** high-speed digital ICs.

× *We have developed PR mapping equipment and <u>applied it to</u> HEMT wafers.*
○ We have developed PR mapping equipment and **used it on** HEMT wafers.

× *Many attempts have been made to <u>apply</u> the microphase-separated domains of block copolymer <u>as</u> a dry-etching mask.*
- 구체적인 사물을 apply 할 수는 없고, [apply] 뒤의 전치사는 [as]가 아니고 [to]이다.

○ Many attempts have been made to **use** the microphase-separated domains of block copolymer **as** a dry-etching mask.

apply의 그 밖의 사용법

룰(rule), 방식(方式), 수자적수순(數字的手順) 등을 실제(實際)에 적용한다.

○ One approach is to **apply** a longest-path **algorithm** to the entire layout.
○ If we **apply** this **model** to carbon doping, then the amount of adsorbed carbon bromide species is determined by...
○ First, we **apply** a smoothing **filter** to the captured image to eliminate stray white and black dots.

…에 전압(電壓), 힘, 압력을 인가(印加) 한다.

○ The ratio increases substantially when an RF **bias is applied**.
○ We carried out simulations to clarify the effects of wafer distortion caused by **pressure applied to** a limited area of a wafer.

액체 등을 물체(物體)의 표면에 바르다.

○ ...**apply** a **coat of resist** to a wafer...
○ Next, we **apply** an anti-reflection coating to the back of the substrate.

기계 등을 가동(稼動) 하다. (주의 : 이 사용법은 기술영어에서는 거의 쓰지 않는다. 또 이 경우 전치사 [to]는 쓰지 말 것.

○ To stop the car, just **apply the brakes**.(브레이크를 걸다)

Space

1. 수치(數値)와 단위(單位)의 약어(略語) 와의 사이에 스페이스를 하나 넣을 것.

× *The power supply was 5V.*

○ The power supply was **5 V**.

× *... at a frequency of 40GHz*

○ ... at a frequency of **40 GHz**

× *The device is 50 μm long.*

○ The device is **50 μm** long.

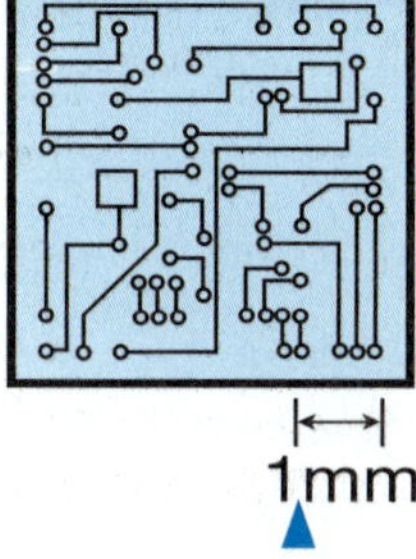

> **NOTE** [수치+단위]를 명사 앞에 놓을 경우, 수치와 단위 사이의 스페이스는 하이픈(-)으로 바뀐다.

○ ... **5-V** operation

○ ... a **40-GHz** signal

○ ... a **50-μm-long** device

2. 수치와 단위의 기호(記號)와의 사이에는 스페이스를 넣지 말 것.

가장 많이 쓰는 기호 : ° ′ ″ % # $ £ ¥

550℃ 55% 6″ $23.50 #7 95°38′23″

3. 괄호 전후에 스페이스를 하나씩 넣을 것.

× *Extreme ultraviolet lithography(EUVL) is a promising way to ...*

○ Extreme ultraviolet lithography **(EUVL)** is a promising way to ...

× *... silicon-on-insulator(SOI) technology...*

○ ... silicon-on -insulator **(SOI)** technology...

× *Three samples(A,B,C) were used to ...*

○ Three samples **(A, B, C)** were used to ...

4. 수식(數式)의 등호(燈號) 또는 부등호(不等號)의 전후에 스페이스를 하나씩 넣을 것.

× *When β=1, the characteristics ...*

○ When **β = 1**, the characteristics ...

5. 그래프의 축(軸)의 변수(變數) 이름과 단위 사이에 스페이스를 하나 넣을 것.

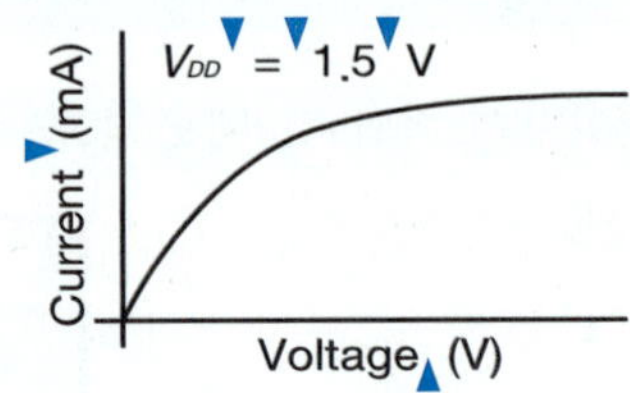

6. 라벨 이름과 숫자 사이에 스페이스를 하나 넣을 것.

× *Figure3*	*Fig.3*	○ Figure 3	Fig. 3
× *Equation(5)*	*Eq.(5)*	○ Equation (5)	Eq. (5)
× *Channel2*	*Ch2*	○ Channel 2	Ch 2

7. 장(章)의 첫머리 리스트의 수치 혹은 문자 뒤에는 스페이스를 하나 또는 둘 넣을 것.

× *1.Introduction*

○ 1. Introduction

8. 참고문헌의 관련 개소(個所)에 적절히 스페이스를 넣을 것.

4. Q. Li, C. Black, and L. D. Farlough, "A 3-GHz Wave-Pipelined Adder," *IEEE Journal of Solid State Circuits*, Vol. 68, No. 5, pp. 517-529, Sept. 1994.

9. 글자 들여쓰기 스타일의 단락(段落)에서 글자 들여쓰기의 표준은 반각(半角) 스페이스 다섯(=한국어 워드프로의 2.5자(字)) 이다.

영어에서는, 기본적인 단락 스타일이 둘 있다.

- **글자 들여쓰기 스타일** : 최초의 행(行)을 5 스페이스 띠우고 단락 사이에 빈 행(行)을 넣지 않는다.
- **블록 스타일** : 글자 들여쓰기를 하지 않고 단락 사이에 빈 행(行)을 일행(一行) 넣는다.

Dynamic Verbs 1

동사는 명사보다 힘이 세다.

다음 한 쌍(pair)의 문장을 음미(吟味) 해 보자.

- Next, the emitter metal was formed by a deposition technique.
  Next, the emitter metal **was deposited**.
- One problem is response time shortening during irradiation.
  One problem is that irradiation **shortens** the response time.

두 쌍의 문장에서도 두 번째 구문(構文)이 쪽이 훨씬 좋다. [Deposit]와 [shorten]이란 동사를 사용함으로써, 문장이 다이나믹해졌다. 또 명사 대신에 동사를 씀으로써 문장이 (짧게 되어) 이해하기 쉽게 되었다.

PRACTICE

고딕체 명사를 동사로 바꾸어라.

1. Hot-electron **injection** was performed on the transistors.

   ____

2. Figure 3 shows an **illustration** of the experimental setup.

   ____

3. Since λ_{out} equals λ_{clock}, a wavelength **conversion operation** from λ_{in} to λ_{out} is accomplished.

   ____

4. The polymer layer **removal** was performed by...

   ____

5. Growth **interruptions** were carried out...

   ____

6. One problem is the bandwidth **limitation** due to the electrical interface.
   One problem is that ____________________________

Prepositions 1

빈칸을 적절한 전치사로 채워라. 만일 필요하다면 x로 매꾸어라.

CHECK YOUR KNOWLEDGE

1. This paper discusses ________ a new approach...
2. X equals ________ Y.
3. X is equal ________ Y.
4. X is the same ________ Y.
5. X is due ________ Y.
6. X consists ________ Y and Z.
7. X influences ________ Y.
8. This section explains ________ the method.
9. X is called ________ Y.
10. X depends ________ Y.

Section 2

Specifying Values

on the contrary

in case of fire

Combining Nouns

contain vs. include

compared to vs. than

that vs. which

Punctuation: Hyphen

Style: Dynamic Verbs 2

Prepositions 2

Specifying Values

POINT

온도나 전압(電壓) 등의 상태량(狀態量)의 수치(數値)를 적을 경우, 그 수치를 상태량 뒤에 붙이는 것이 보통이다. 즉, 아래와 같은 표현은 별로 쓰이지 않는다.

× *...at a 325℃ temperature*

× *...at over-10-Gbit/s data rates*

a + 단수명사 + 전치사 (of,...) + 수치

a temperature of 325℃

- ... a transistor with **a** gate length **of** 0.6㎛ ...
- Measurements were made at a θ **of** 23°.
  - 위 문장에서 보듯이, 이 패턴은 기호에도 적용된다.
- The power dissipation is 1.3W at **a** V_{DD} **of** 3.3 V.
- The stage moves through **a** distance **of** 125 mm
- Figure 3 shows simulation results for **a** voltage **of** 2 V.
- The Huffman coding modules have **a** throughput **of** over 10 MOPS.
  - 위의 문장에서 over는 형용사이며, 전치사가 아닌 것에 주의 하라. 밑줄 그어진 부분은 **a** throughput **of** more than 10 MOPS 과 마찬가지이다.

복수(複數)명사 + 전치사 (of, ...) + 수치

the temperatures of 240℃ and 325℃

- We annealed the wafers at temperatures **between** 600℃ and 900℃.
- Growth temperatures **above** 500℃ enhance the desorption of ...
- It operates at speeds **of** up to 2.6 Gbit/s.
- We used drain voltages **of** 0.1 V and 2 V for nMOSFETs.
- At light intensities **above** about 100 W/m², MTP4 has a greater ...

콤마, 괄호, 콜론

수치의 개수(個數)가 특정(特定) 한 경우, 콤마(,), 또는 괄호(( )) 혹은 콜론(:)을 쓴다.

- This circuit used **two** supply voltages, 3.3 V and 2 V, and has ...
- This circuit used **two** supply voltages(3.3 V, 2 V), and has ...

NOTE 리스트는 괄호로 에워싸인 경우, [and]를 쓸 필요는 없다.

- This circuit uses **two** supply voltages: 3.3 V and 2 V.

수치 + 단위 (Space)	수치 + 단위약어(略語) (Space)	수치 + 기호 (No space)
영어에서는 수(數)를 단어로써 취급하기 때문에 수와 그 다음 단어 사이에 스페이스를 넣을 것.	영어에서는 약어(略語)를 단어로 취급하기 때문에, 수와 그 다음 약어 사이에 스페이스를 넣을 것.	영어에서는 기호는 단어로 취급하지 않기 때문에 수와 그 다음 기호 사이에는 스페이스를 넣지 말것.
7 degrees Celsius	7 deg. Celsius	7℃
6 inches	6 in.	6″
24 nanometers	24 nm	
1.4 volts	1.4 V	
8 micrometers	8 mm	
2.4 gigahertz	2.4 GHz	
96 percent		96%
23 dollars		$23

가장 많이 쓰는 기호 : ° ′ ″ % # $ £ ¥

on the contrary

POINT

[On the contrary]는 직전(直前)에 말했던 것에 비해 단지 무엇인가가 다른 것을 말할 경우에는 쓰지 않는다. 직전에 말했던 것이 틀렸다고 주장하기 위해 쓴다.

MISTAKE (틀림)

CORRECTION (정정(訂正))

DEFINITION: 지금 말했던 것에 관해 전혀 찬성을 못하거나, 반대하는 경우, [On the contrary]를 쓴다. [이것과는 반대로]

기술영어에서는, 이런 표현은 거의 쓰이지 않는다.

GOOD EXAMPLES

- A: Everyone can certainly afford soap to take a bath.
  B: **On the contrary**, a great number of people in India and elsewhere cannot even buy enough food!

- Of course, I' m not saying that this type of transistor is useless. **On the contrary**, I think it is one of the most promising designs.

DEFINITION: 다음에 말하는 것이, 직전에 말한 것과 크게 다른 경우, [in contrast], [in contrast to] 또는 [by contrast]라는 표현을 쓴다. 그것과는 대조적으로, ... 와 달리]

in contrast (to) by contrast

TYPICAL MISTAKES

× *For Process C, the current decreases between the first and second measurement. On the contrary, there is no change for Process D.*

○ For process C, the current decreases between the first and second measurement. **In contrast**, there is no change for Process D.

× *The surface of the cathode was very smooth and there was no apparent damage. On the contrary, parts of the anode stuck to the separator and the surface was rough.*

○ The surface of the cathode was very smooth and there was no apparent damage. **In contrast**, parts of the anode stuck to the separator and the surface was rough.

GOOD EXAMPLES

○ Many Type-A devices failed in less than 100 hours. **In contrast**, only one Type-B device failed in 750 hours.

○ **In contrast to** the static analysis at the architectural level, at this level we analyzed the dynamic features of the encoding.

○ The HIZ Group in Germany uses compound-semiconductor waveguides. **In contrast**, our optical interconnections consist of SiO_2 and polymer.

○ The capacitor keeps the supply voltage under −45 V. **In contrast**, without a capacitor the supply voltage exceeds −30 V.

in case of fire

POINT

[In case] 또는 [in case of]는 이상(異狀)이 생기는 경우에만 쓰인다. 한국어의 경우는 [for] 또는 [when] 으로 번역한다.

DEFINITION: [In case of]는, 특별한 상황(狀況)에서 무엇을 해야하는가를 나타내는 것이며, 공식적 게시(揭示)에 쓰이고 있다. [... 의 경우에는, ... 할 때는]

- **In case of emergency**, call 119.

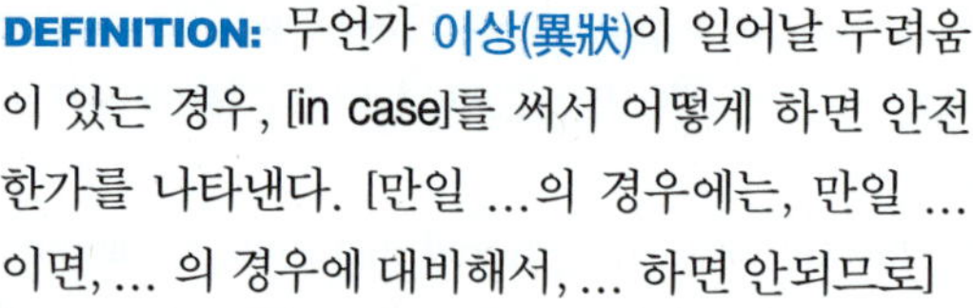

DEFINITION: 무언가 이상(異狀)이 일어날 두려움이 있는 경우, [in case]를 써서 어떻게 하면 안전한가를 나타낸다. [만일 ...의 경우에는, 만일 ... 이면, ... 의 경우에 대비해서, ... 하면 안되므로]

- Take a map **in case** you get lost.
- Here is my telephone number **in case** you need to call me.

DEFINITION: 보통 케이스와 다른 개별적(個別的) 처리 방법 등을, [in the case of]를 써서 나타낸다. [···에 관해 말하면, ···에 관해서는]

- In the U.S., it takes 4 years to graduate from university, or 5 **in the case of** premed students.
  [*premed student* = 메디칼 스쿨 예과 학생]
- Every one who gets on the bus must pay the fare, except **in the case of** a woman carrying a baby, where the baby is free.

기술영어에서는 이 세 가지 표현을 거의 쓰지 않는다.

NOTE [In case], [in case of] 또는 [in the case of] 대신에, [for] 또는 [when]을 써서 조건을 나타낸다.

~~in case ...~~  **for**

× *<u>In case of</u> smaller circuits, SIMOX devices are 25% to 50% faster than bulk ones.*

• [만일 회로(回路)가 훨씬 더 작다면]이란 의미가 되어 버린다.

○ **For** smaller circuits, SIMOX devices are 25% to 50% faster than bulk ones.

× *This is the calculated waveform <u>In the case of</u> ideal boundary conditions.*

○ This is the calculated waveform **for** ideal boundary conditions.

× *Figure 5 shows results <u>in case of</u> a data rate of 1 GBit/s.*

○ Figure 5 shows results **for** a data rate of 1 GBit/s.

~~in case ...~~  **when**

× *WSiN makes a good barrier layer <u>in case</u> an RF bias is applied during formation.*

○ WSiN makes a good barrier layer **when** an RF bias is applied during formation.

× *<u>In case</u> a positive bias is applied to the electrode, ions are deposited only at defect sites.*

○ **When** a positive bias is applied to the electrode, ions are deposited only at defect sites.

PRACTICE

아래의 본보기에 따라 [for] 또는 [when]을 써서 괄호안의 조건을 문장에 추가하라. 또 필요에 따라, =, 〈, 〉 등의 수학 기호도 영어 표현으로 고쳐라.

Examples:

The flow rates were 6 sccm (SF_6) and 4 sccm(CF_4).

→ The flow rates were 6 sccm **for SF_6** and 4 sccm **for CF_4**.

(Si layer, thick), we get simple periodic oscillations.

→ **When the Si layer is thick**, we get simple periodic oscillations.

1. The values are 8.4 mW (Device A) and 11.2 mW (Device B).

____ .

2. This phenomenon appears only (the input power > a certain value).

____ .

3. This figure shows pulse patterns (output voltage, 200 mV).

____ .

4. (the numerical aperture, low), V_b has no effect.

____ .

5. These figures show the performance (156-Mbit/s signals).

____ .

6. The resistivity increased monotonically with annealing time (zirconium layer, 200 nm thick).

____ .

7. (total thickness > $1 \mu m$), the coupling efficiency is much larger.

____ .

8. Chemical polishing reduces the threshold voltage (long-channel devices).

____ .

9. (a defect is completely within the silicon), it does not give rise to a gate oxide defect.

____ .

10. (thin barriers), IRIT increases with barrier thickness.

____ .

Combining Nouns

다음과 같이 명사 앞에 명사를 두는 일이 있다.

○ **stone** wall

○ **Adidas leather tennis** shoes

이 경우, 앞에 있는 명사가 뒤에 있는 명사의 종류, 특성 등을 나타낸다.

그러나 다음 표현은 맞지 않다.

× *the room wall*

위의 예에서는 room은 wall의 종류가 아니기 때문에 wall의 수식(修飾)이 되어, 실제로 wall은 room의 일부분이기 때문에 이 표현은 틀렸다.

's의 사용법도 자주 틀린다.

× *the room's wall*

이 표현은 맞지 않다. 영어에서는 [어포스트로피+s] 라는 표현법은 주로 **인간** 또는 **시간**의 경우에만 쓰인다. (예를 들면, Bob's coat, today's newspaper)

맞는 표현은 다음과 같다.

○ the wall **of** the room

또, 많은 명사를 겹친 표현은 흔히 이해하기 어려워, 피하는 편이 좋다.

× interlayer dielectric water molecule behavior

○ the behavior **of** water molecules **in** interlayer dielectrics

아래의 경우, [of] 또는 [in]을 쓴다.

Components, parts, etc. (구성요소, 부분 등)

the inner wall **of** the hole

the top **of** the valence band

the interface circuits **of** LSIs

the surface **of** the resist

each stage **of** the amplifier

Properties (특성)

the thickness **of** the layer

the resistivity **of** the via plugs

the amplitude **of** the vibrations

the slope **of** the line

the electrochemical behavior **of** a Ca counter electrode

Changes (변화)

NOTE an increase in the voltage of 5 V

[In]은 변화하는 **상태량(狀態量)**을 나타낸다

[of]는 그 **변화의 정도**를 나타낸다.

이 경우, "a 5-V increase **in** the voltage" 라고 표현해도 좋다.

an increase **in** the current
the gradual decrease **in** the gain
a 20% change **in** the resistance
the variation **in** width
fluctuations **in** the voltage
the degradation **in** quality

Procedures, processes, etc. (수순(手順), 과정(過程) 등)

the calculation **of** very small values
the regeneration **of** optical signals
the etching **of** contact holes
estimation **of** the base resistance
measurement **of** the optical properties
control **of** the exposure conditions

Number, amount, size, etc (수, 양, 사이즈 등)

the number **of** circuits
the amount **of** impact ionization
the increasing size **of** wafers
the degree **of** copper contamination
the percentage **of** people with allergies

Mathematical operations (수학연산(數學演算))

the sum **of** the fundamental and third-harmonic components
the product **of** n^2 and the length
the ratio **of** X to Y

NOTE 각 과학분야에서 쓰이는 표현은, 단축된 고유명사로서 사용되기 위해서, 그 표준적조합(標準的組合)을 그 분야의 관습(慣習)에 따라 써야 한다. 이러한 표현은 흔히 짧고, 두 단어의 조합으로 되어 있다. 관련 분야의 논문 등을 조사하여, 그러한 표현을 보고 외워두자.

gate length
line width or linewidth
crystal quality
hole concentration
substrate temperature
signal-to-noise ratio, S/N ratio

PRACTICE

본보기에 따라, 다음 문장에 적절한 전치사를 넣어라.

Examples:

a new contact hole etching method	→ a new method **of** etching contract holes
the oxide quality degradation	→ the degradation **in** the quality **of** the oxide
the field oxide edge	→ the edge **of** the field oxide

1. the Si-Si bond length

 ____

2. the critical-dimension change

 ____

3. intensity profile calculation and pattern profile calculation

 ____

4. the mirror scanning frequency

 ____

5. the GaAs buffer layer thickness

 ____

6. sub-100-nm pattern replication

 ____

7. small-contact-hole etching

 ____

8. at less-than-10-Mbit/s coding rates

 ____

9. surface-acid amount control method

 ____

contain vs. include

POINT

어떤 것이 라는 것에 포함 되어 있는 경우, [contain]은 가장 단순(單純)하게, **기본적인** 이미지를 나타낸다. [include]를 쓰면, 특별한 **뉘앙스**를 띈다.

contain

DEFINITION: X contains A는, A가 X에 들어 있음을 가리킨다.

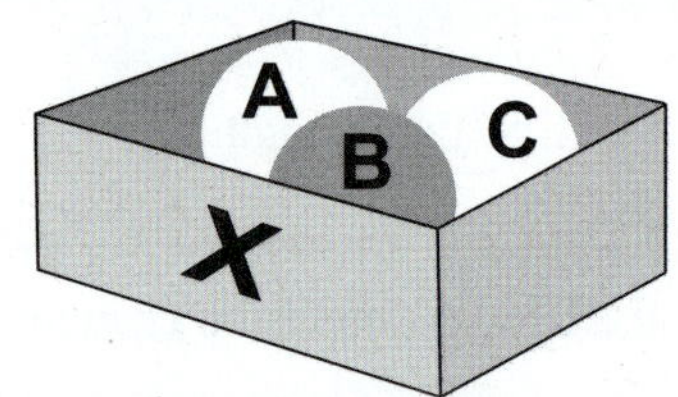

NOTE [X contains A]란 표현을 쓰는 경우, X에 A만이 포함되어 있는지 아닌가에 관해서는 신경쓰지 않는다. 윗 그림처럼, [X contains A]에 대하여 [X contains A and B] 및 [X contains A, B, and C]라는 표현도 맞다.

GOOD EXAMPLES

○ Type-A film **contains** more water than Type-B film.
- A 타입의 필름은, B 타입의 필름에 비하여 물을 많이 포함하고 있다.

○ Each device **contains** a single nanometer-sized island.
- 각 디바이스에 나노사이즈의 [섬]이 하나만 존재한다.

○ The batteries should **not contain** any toxic substances.
- 전지에는 유독물질이 존재해서는 안 된다.

○ Fingerprint images usually **contain** stray black and white dots.
- 지문(指紋) 이미지에는 흔히 불규칙적인 흑백(黑白) 점들이 들어 있다.

include (1)

DEFINITION: 먼저 **어떤 그룹**에 언급(言及)한 후, 그것에 포함된 일부 혹은 전부를 [include]를 써서 **리스트업** 할 수가 있다.

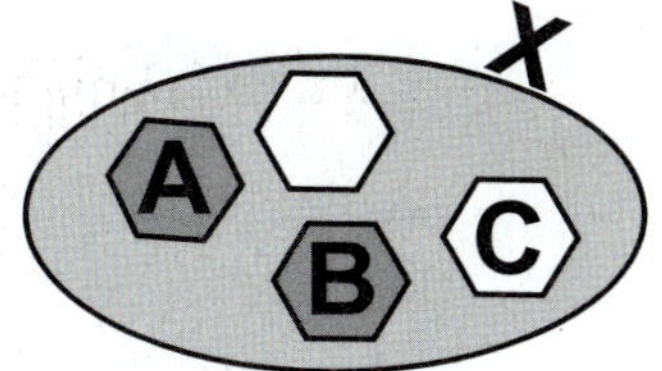

GOOD EXAMPLES

- There are several large cities in Japan. They **include** Tokyo, Osaka, and Fukuoka.
  특정한 그룹
- The next topic is patterning characteristics under actual LSI fabrication conditions. These **include** resolution, mask linearity, critical-dimension control, and exposure latitude.
- The materials used to make optical waveguides **include** semiconductors, organics, and glasses.

include (2)

DEFINITION: X includes B 란, 다른 것 (특히 설명이 필요 없는)에 더하여 B도 X에 들어 있음을 가리킨다.

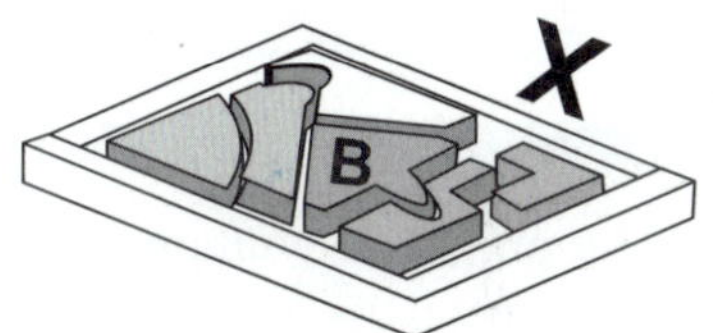

GOOD EXAMPLES

- The test setup **included** a newly developed circuit.
  - 시험장치에는, (표준적인 부분에 더하여) 새로 개발한 회로도 들어 있다.
- The module **includes** a Peltier device.
- This unit **includes** an AC/DC converter.
  - 이 유니트의 표준적 구성요소에 더하여, AC/DC 컨버터도 이 유니트에 포함되어 있다.

include (3)

DEFINITION: A를 X에 include 한다. **또는** A가 X에 include 된다는 것은, **일부러** A를 X에 넣는 것을 의미한다.

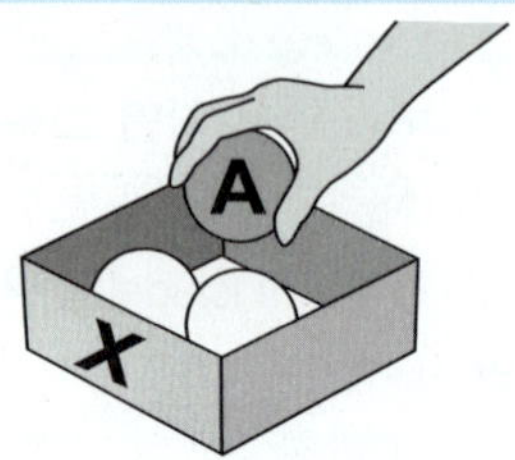

GOOD EXAMPLES

- For comparison, some previously reported data **are included** in the graph.
- There is also a polymer overcladding, but **I did not include** it in this diagram.
- For simplicity, no compensation circuits **were included**.

include (4)

DEFINITION: **전체**의 양을 말한 뒤, 어떤 양(量)은 별개의 것이 아니라, 그 **일부**임을 설명하는데는 [include]를 쓴다.

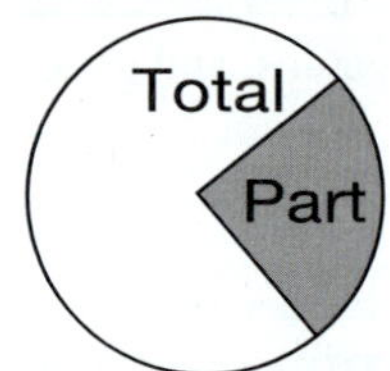

GOOD EXAMPLES

- The programs contain about 300,000 lines of code, **including** the 100,000 lines that we provided.
  - 전부 300,000행(行)의 프로그램 중, 우리는 100,000행을 작성(作成)하고, 다른 사람은 나머지 200,000행을 작성 했다.
- The timing jitter was less than 800 femtoseconds. This **includes** measurement instrument jitter.

PRACTICE

[Contain]이나 [include], 또는 두 쪽을 써서 빈칸을 메워라. 양쪽을 쓰는 경우, 그 의미의 차이에 주의하라.

1. Since this box ____________ only two books, it is very light.
2. The development took 9 months, ____________ *ing* testing.
3. I haven' t ____________ them in the diagram to keep things simple.
4. This large structure in the crystal ________________ an extremely large void(=empty space).
5. To check the fabrication process, small test elements are ____________ on a chip.
6. These devices all ____________ 50 transistors.
7. Next, some results for a fabricated device are presented. These __________ the conversion gain, intermodulation distortion ratio, and noise figure.
8. We estimated the switching time to be 60 ps, which ____________ the 50-ps rise time of the electrical pulse generator. (ps=picosecond)
9. These equations ____________ very complex operations.
10. The buried oxide is 103 nm thick, ________________ ing a 20-nm-thick ITOX layer.
11. Possible applications ____________ satellite broadcasting and cable TV.
12. This structure has several advantages, _________________ *ing* reduced parasitic capacitances and simple device isolation.
13. The chips _______________ 320,000 transistors.
14. A transistor _______________ both n- and p-type regions.
15. Eighteen masks are used in the lithography. This number does not ________________ the ones for wiring.
16. These wafers went through our LSI fabrication process, which _________ plasma etching, implantation doping, and so on.
17. The drain saturation current of an nMOSFET ____________ the parasitic bipolar current.

compared to vs. than

비교하는 경우 흔히 비교형(-er than)을 쓴다.

× *X has a higher density compared to Y.*

○ X has a **higher density than** Y.

○ X is **denser than** Y.

× *The bandwidth of X is improved by 75% compared to that of Y.*

○ The bandwidth of X is 75% **larger than** that of Y.

비교의 기준을 나타내는 경우 [compared to/with]를 쓴다.

[개는 큽니까. 아니면 작습니까?]

이 질문은, 비교의 표준을 보여주지 않는 한, 무의미 하다.

A dog is **big**, **compared to** a mouse.

NOTE [Bigger]가 아니고, [big]이다.

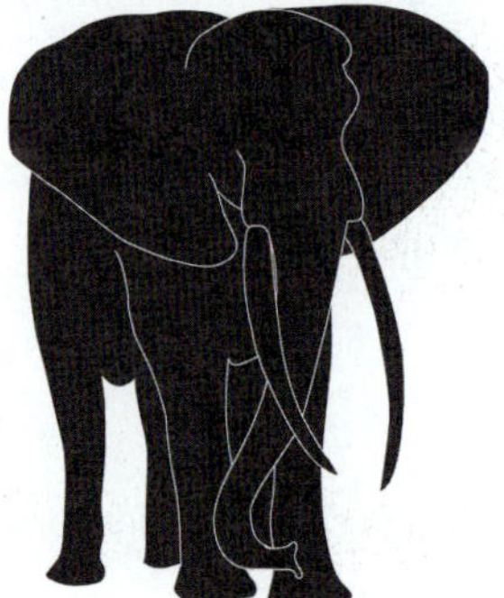

NOTE [Smaller]가 아니고, [small]이다.

A dog is **small**, compared to an elephant.

GOOD EXAMPLES

○ The grains in the crystal are relatively **small, compared to** those of the reference sample.

○ The diffusion length of zinc is **negligible, compared with** the size of the device.

○ **Compared with** xylene, ester acetates have a rather **low** sensitivity; but they provide better contrast.

○ The thermal resistance is 660 Ω/W. This value is among the lowest for Type-A devices; but it is still **large, compared to** the 80-300 Ω/W for Type-B devices.

PRACTICE

[Compared] 또는 [comparison]을 삭제하다.

NOTE 형용사를 강조할 때, [very big] 처럼 [very]를 자주 쓴다. 비교행의 경우, 강조할 때, [much bigger] 또는 [much more beautiful]처럼 [much]를 쓴다.

1. This method is **very effective** <u>compared to</u> conventional ones.

   ______________________________.

2. The processing power is **very low** <u>in comparison with</u> that of conventional machines.

   ______________________________.

3. The efficiency is **very small** <u>compared to</u> that of the other devices.

   ______________________________.

4. The current gains are **very high** <u>compared to</u> this value.

   ______________________________.

5. The size of the new circuit is **reduced by about 25%** <u>compared with</u> that of a conventional one.

   ______________________________.

6. The accuracy is **lower** <u>compared to</u> that of the simulation results.

   ______________________________.

that vs. which

[That]로 시작하는 형용사절(節)은 [that]앞의 명사가 무엇을 가리키는가를 명확히 하기 위해 쓴다. [That] 앞에 콤마는 넣지 말것.

○ In this area, there are <u>two shops</u> **that** sell computers.

That 절을 생략하면, 어떻게 되는지 보라.

× *In this area, there are <u>two shops</u>.*

의미가 완전히 변하여, 이 상점이 무슨 상점인지 알 수 없게 된다. 더구나, 이 근처에 상점이 두 개 이상 있으면, 이 문장은 맞지 않다. 따라서 가리키는 상점을 명확히 하기위해 that절은 불가결(不可缺) 하다.

GOOD EXAMPLES

○ There are three kinds of lasers **that** <u>are tuned by means of the injection current.</u>

○ We need a <u>design tool</u> **that** <u>can properly handle the propagation of both light waves and microwaves</u>.

○ The power **that** <u>can be generated by green energy sources</u> is on the order of milliwatts.

[Which]로 시작하는 형용사절은, 어느 사물에 관해 더 많은 정보를 제공하기 위해 쓴다. [Which] 앞에 콤마를 넣을 것.

○ That shop, **which** sells computers, was built recently.

Which 절을 생략하면 어떻게 되는지 보라.

○ That shop was built recently.

이 문장의 기본적 의미는 바뀌지 않는다. 그 때문에 which 절은 불가결한 것이 아니고, 더 많은 정보를 제공하고 있을 뿐이다.

GOOD EXAMPLES

- One way to identify an authorized user is to employ biometrics, **which** relies on people' s unique physical characteristics.
- Figure 7 shows the configuration of the receiver system, **which** employs a PD-EAM as a demultiplexer.
  - 이 경우 [the]는 [앞에 말한 것]이란 의미로, 독자는 어떤 시스템인지 이미 알고 있다. 한편, 이 시스템을 처음으로 소개하는 경우는 [the]를 [a]로, 그래서 [which]를 [that][로 바꾸지 않으면 안 된다.

- Figure 7 shows the configuration of **a** receiver system **that** employs a PD-EAM as a demultiplexer.
- The signals are fed into the second AWG, **which** combines them.
- The modulators exhibited good BER performance on all 80 channels, **which** have a spacing of 50 GHz.

- Hyphen -

하이픈이 없는 경우, 형용사는 마지막 명사를 수식한다.

Red wind bottles are red.
(=red bottles for wine)

명사 앞에 쓰인 구(句)중의 단어와의 관련(關聯)을 나타낼 경우, 하이픈을 쓴다.

Red-wind bottles are usually green.
(=bottles for red wind)

NOTE 명사 앞에 두는 명사는 단수형이다.
× *Red-wines bottles are ...*

NOTE 일반적으로, 마지막 명사 앞에는 하이픈을 쓰지 않는다.
× *Red-wine-bottles are ...*

1. 수-명사 [명사는 단수형]

3 computer systems

a **3-computer** system
(× *a 3-computer**s** system*)

a 3-bedroom apartment
2-input NAND gates
a 3-region model

a 50,000-word dictionary
a two-step process
six-stage distributed amplifiers

2. 수 - 단위(單位) - 형용사 [단위는 단수형]

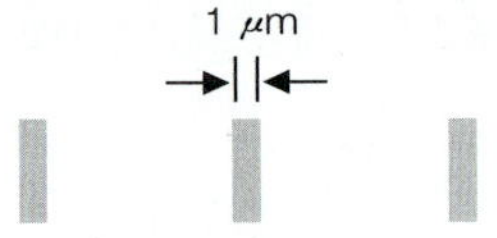

3 micron-wide lines
(= 3 1-micron-wide lines)

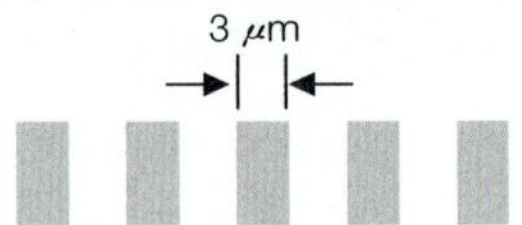

3-micron-wide lines
(× *3-micron**s**-wide lines*)

a 6-year-old child
6-inch wafers
0.3-μm L&S patterns
10-Gbit/s interconnections
40-GHz optical signals
3-ps pulses

3. 형용사 - 명사 [명사는 단수형]

a high-temperature process
high-energy photons
short-channel effects
paired-net routing
a low soft-error rate
a bird's-eye view
short-gate-length FETs
low-power, high-speed VLSIs
high-quality wafers
real-time processing

4. 명사 - 형용사 [명사는 단수형]

cross-sectional view
error-free operation
hot-carrier-induced degradation
a mirror-polished surface
surface-illuminated p-i-n photodiodes
a mode-locked laser

5. 기타

time-space conversion
electron-hole pair
on-wafer probe
via-to-via pitch
state-of-the-are technology
current-voltage characteristics
on-demand manufacturing
analog-to digital converter

NOTE 하이픈이 있는 표현을 리스트업하는 경우, 하이픈을 그대로 남겨둘 필요가 있다.

zero-dimensional and two-dimensional structures
→ zero- and two-dimensional structures

3- μm-wide, 5- μm-wide, and 7- μm-wide lines
→ 3-, 5-, and 7- μm-wide lines

PRACTICE

다음 문장에는 틀린 것이 있다. 틀린 것을 찾아 내어 고쳐라.

1. ... a 15-minutes presentation ...
2. ... a gate-width of 5 μm ...
3. We made 3-micron long devices.
4. We made 3-microns-long devices.
5. we made 3-micron-long devices.
6. We made a device 3 μm long.
7. We made a device 3- μm-long.
8. ... a silicon-on-insulator substrate ...
9. ... a thick buffer layer ...
10. ... high temperature superconductors ...
11. a one dimensional system
12. a high oversampling frequency of 6-MHz
13. a 1-V power supply
14. a GaAs buffer layer 480-nm thick
15. a 0.5 thick layer of resist
16. lattice matched substrates
17. a low voltage LSI
18. a low voltage level
19. at a low-V_{th}

Dynamic Verbs 2

능동태(能動態)는 수동태(受動態) 보다 설득력이 있다.

다음 예를 생각해 보자.

- The electrical characteristics **are not changed** by adding the intermediate layers.
- The intermediate layers **do not change** the electrical characteristics.

두 번째 문장은 간결 · 단순하며, 또 명백하고 직접적(直接的)이다. 그것은 능동태의 힘을 보여주고 있다.

PRACTICE

밑줄 그어진 동사를 능동태로 바꾸어라. 단, 주어는 고딕체로 나와 있다.

1. In **the calculations**, these atoms <u>are taken</u> into account.

   ____

2. Mechanical stress <u>is generated by</u> **wire bonding**.

   ____

3. The optical signal <u>was focused on</u> the device with **a lens**.

   ____

4. The output jitter <u>is suppressed by</u> **our circuit technique**.

   ____

5. The characteristics <u>are</u> dramatically <u>improved by</u> **the feedback**.

   ____

6. The conduction band is raised by **the thin p+ layer**.

____

7. In **this electrical excitation**, ballistic electrons are generated in the diodes.

____

8. In **this model**, the gate-drain capacitance is included.

____

9. By **using this circuit**, the number of connections are reduced by 75%.

____

Prepositions 2

빈칸을 적절한 전치사로 메꾸어라. 만일 필요하다면, X로 메꾸어라.

REVIEW

a. X is due ___________ Y.

b. X influences ___________ Y.

c. X equals ___________ Y.

d. This paper discusses ___________ a new approach...

e. X is the same ___________ Y.

CHECK YOUR KNOWLEDGE

1. X is independent ___________ Y.
2. X has an influence ___________ Y.
3. X causes ___________ Y.
4. X is identical ___________ Y.
5. X is equivalent ___________ Y.
6. Result X agrees ___________ result Y.
7. X affects ___________ Y.
8. X has an effect ___________ Y.
9. X is suitable ___________ Y.
10. X is composed ___________ Y and Z.

Section 3

for -ing

is expected

can, could

as a result

is thought

becomes vs. is

remarkable

Punctuation: Colon

Style: Unnecessary Repetition

Prepositions 3

for -ing

POINT

I went to the store for buying bread.
이 문장은 영어 답지가 않다.

동작의 목적을 나타내는 경우, 오른쪽 표현을 쓴다.

to + 동사 (=목적을 나타내는 부정사)
in order to + 동사
so that, etc.

○ I went to the store
- to buy bread.
- in order to buy bread.
- so that I could buy bread.

TYPICAL MISTAKES

× *For fabricating the devices, we selected UV-curable resin.*
- [For -ing]으로 문장을 시작하는 것은 자주 보이는 잘못이다.

○ **To fabricate** the devices, we selected UV-curable resin.

× *We developed a new correction method for improving the pattern placement accuracy.*

○ We developed a new correction method **to improve** the pattern placement accuracy.

× *We need this type of material for getting good performance.*

○ We need this type ;of material **to get** good performance.

사물의 용도를 나타내는 경우, [for -ing]을 쓸 수가 있다.

GOOD EXAMPLES

○ This is a **lens for focusing** light.

○ A simple analytical **model for predicting** gate-drain breakdown voltage is presented.

○ This is a useful **technique for forming** the absorption layer.

NOTE [동사 + for], 예를 들면 thank someone for (doing) something 및 be used for 등과 같은 숙어(熟語)는 위 논의(議論)의 밖이다.

○ The authors wish to **thank** K. Suzuki **for making** the X-ray masks.

PRACTICE

다음 문장에서 올바른 것을 뽑고 틀린 것은 고쳐라.

1. In this LSI, four metal layers are used <u>for wiring</u>.
2. We have developed a technology <u>for combining</u> very small LSIs and devices with larger feature sizes on a chip.
3. <u>For measuring</u> the resistance, the alloy and the cathode were attached to a platinum mesh.
4. A thermoelectric cooler was added <u>for controlling</u> the temperature of the chip.
5. <u>For tracking</u> moving objects, it is necessary to match key features in neighboring frames.
6. A wide tuning range is required <u>for reducing</u> system costs.
7. Figure 3 shows a frame <u>for supporting</u> 16 fibers. [frame= 틀]
8. This section describes the experiments we performed <u>for verifying</u> the proper operation of the device.
9. We optimized the laser itself <u>for improving</u> the performance of the laser array.
10. We used a laser pointer as an ideal device <u>for pointing</u>.
11. Atomic-force microscopy is now widely used <u>for examining</u> surface structures.
12. The composition of the WSiN was measured <u>for assessing</u> the effect of an RF bias.
13. This section describes pulse-pattern generators <u>for testing</u> ultrafast ICs.
14. The exposure dose needed <u>for patterning</u> is inversely proportional to the degree of dissociation.

is expected

POINT

저자(著者)가 개인적으로 expect 한 것 뿐이라면, 이 표현은 쓰지 않고 [should]를 쓴다.

기대된다

DEFINITION: 무엇인가가 is expected 라면, **많은 사람**은 그것이 일어나리라고 예상할 수 있다. 즉, 그것이 일어날 가능성이 **일반적으로 받아들여지고 있다.**

기술영어에서는 [be expected]는 별로 쓰이지 않는다.

GOOD EXAMPLES

- The trend toward further device miniaturization **is expected to** continue.
  - 누구든 트랜지스터가 작게 되리라고 믿고 있다.
- VUV lithography **is expected to be used** for the fabrication of devices at the 100-and 70-nm technology nodes.
  - 이 분야의 거의 모든 연구자는 그렇게 믿고 있다.
- With the advent of the network computing era, the number and variety of mobile units **are expected to increase** greatly.
- Ultralow-voltage circuit technology **is expected to pave the way** to mobile solar-cell systems.

~~is expected~~
~~is expected to~~
~~is expected that~~
~~is expected for~~
~~is expected as~~

TYPICAL MISTAKES

× *This device <u>is expected to operate</u> at high bit rates of over 40 Gbit/s.*

- 이 디바이스를 작성(作成)한 연구자 본인만이 그렇게 생각하고 있기 때문에, 일반적으로 받아들여지고 있다고 여겨지지 않는다.

○ This device **should operate** at high bit rates of over 40 Gbit/s.

× *examining this region <u>is expected to give</u> us a clue to the behavior of the ethoxy group (C_2H_5O).*

○ Examining this region **should give** us a clue to the behavior of the ethoxy group (C_2H_5O).

× *When these polymers aggregate, <u>it is expected that</u> they become smaller.*

○ When these polymers aggregate, they **should** become smaller.

× *Due to the high electron velocity of these materials, high-speed operation <u>is expected</u>.*

○ The high electron velocity of these materials **should enable** devices to operate at very high speeds.

× *The resonant tunneling diode <u>is expected as</u> the most useful quantum effect device.*

○ The resonant tunneling diode is the most **promising** quantum effect device. [promising=기대되는]

NOTE 여기서 문제가 되어 있는 것은 [be expected]이며, 아래의 [expected]의 쓰임새에는 특히 문제는 없다.

○ The intensity is much **lower than expected**.

○ These data show the resolution **expected from** Eq. (1).

○ The measured value is **smaller than that expected from** the simulation.

○ If the slope errors were comparable to this value, **the expected** exposure characteristics would not be obtained at all.

○ **As expected**, the ratio slowly drops as time passes.

can, could

Ex. 1 : 먼저 다음 문장을 생각해 보자.

- Bob **can run** the 100-meter dash in 10 seconds. (봅은 100미터 달리기를 10초에 달릴수가 있다.)
  이 문장에 관해, 다음과 같은 질문이 생긴다.
  - 정말? 봅은 실제로 100미터 달리기를 한 일이 있는가?
  - 왜 10초
  - 그것은 사실인 증거가 있는가가, 그렇찮으면, 쓸모 없는 자만(自慢) 하는 말인가?

다음에 아래의 [사실을 말한] 문장을 생각하라.

- Bob **ran** the 100-meter dash in 10 seconds. (봅은 100미터 달리기를 10초에 달렸다.)
  이 기술(記述)에는, 다음과 같은 것에 의문의 여지가 없다.
  1. 봅이 그것을 해낼 가능성이 있다.
  2. 봅은 그것을 할 능력이 있다.

Ex. 2 : 다음 문장의 다름을 음미해 보라.
The sun can rise in the east. (태양은 동쪽에서 뜰 가능성이 있다.)
The sun rises in the east. (태양은 동쪽에서 떠오른다.)

NOTE 일어날 가능성이 있다는 것은, 일어나지 않을 가능성도 있다는 것이다. 그러므로, 실제로 일어난 것에는 [can]은 쓰이지 않는다.

일반적으로, 연구결과, 발견, 관찰 및 결론을 [can]이나 [could]를 써서 말하기 보다는 사실로서 말하는 쪽이 훨씬 더 설득력이 있다.

TYPICAL MISTAKES

다음 표현에 특히 주의를 기울인다.

~~can/could achieve~~  achieved

× *We can achieve a high coupling efficiency of over 70%.*
  - 가능성? 어떤 조건을 바탕으로 해서?

○ We **achieved** a high coupling efficiency of over 70%. (Fact!)

× *We could achieve a large tolerance of about 50 .*

○ We **achieved** a large tolerance of about 50 . (Fact!)

~~can/could obtain~~  **obtain**

× *For the quarter-micron SOI process, we can obtain a delay time of 10 ns at a voltage of 0.5 V.* (가능성?)

○ For the quarter-micron SOI process, we **obtained** a delay time of 10 ns at a voltage of 0.5 V. (Fact!)

× *By optimizing the O_2 flow rate, we could obtain high-quality films.*

○ By optimizing the O_2 flow rate, we **obtained** high-quality films. (Fact!)

× *A dynamic range of over 28 dB could be obtained for both modules.*

○ A dynamic range of over 28 dB **was obtained** for both modules. (Fact!)

~~can/could observe~~  **observed**

× *We could observe a melted region on the input facet.*

○ We **observed** a melted region on the input facet. (Fact!)

× *We have recently developed a DBR laser that can provide a mode-hop-free tuning range of more than 6 nm.*

- 그렇게 될 수도, 안 될수도 있는 것인가?

○ We have recently developed a DBR laser that **provides** a mode-hop-free tuning range of more than 6 nm. (Fact!)

× *This HEMT can satisfy the requirements for 100-Gbit/s ICs.*

- 그렇게 안 될 가능성도 있다!

○ This HEMT **satisfies** the requirements for 100-Gbit/s ICs. (Fact!)

× *Each microlens could be formed at the correct position.*

○ Each microlens **was formed** at the correct position. (Fact!)

× *The circuit could generate an ultrafast electrical pulse.*

○ The circuit **generated** an ultrafast electrical pulse. (Fact!)

× *We could demonstrate the continuous-wave (CW) operation of the LDs at room temperature.*

○ We **demonstrated** the continuous-wave (CW) operation of the LDs at room temperature. (Fact!)

× *The median lifetime could be calculated from the activation energy.*

○ The median lifetime **was calculated** from the activation energy. (Fact!)

GOOD EXAMPLES

- This device **can produce** a conversion gain if an intense pump beam is injected.
  - 능력(필요하면, 이 디바이스는 변환(變換) 게인을 발생할 수 있다.
- Millimeter-wave signals **can be generated** at a frequencies of up to 240 GHz by using a mode-locked laser.
  - 가능성(가능성의 한계를 나타낸다.)
- We think we **can increase** the output power by optimizing the antenna design.
  - 가능성(출력파워를 증가하는 것이 가능하지만, 그것에 관해 절대적 확신은 갖고 있지 않다.)

PRACTICE

다음 문장에서 맞는 것을 골라라.

1. The good agreement between the experimental and simulation results **can demonstrate** that the simulation method is correct.
2. These switches **can operate** at bit rates as high as 20 Gbit/s.
3. We **can use** either Method A or Method B to make the device.
4. The resolution **can be estimated to be** 0.19 nm from the dimensions of the device.
5. This fabrication technique **can prevent** the unintentional formation of parasitic islands.
6. We investigated whether or not WSiN **can prevent** copper diffusion.
7. **There can be** three possibilities: (a) no diode switches; (b) one diode switches; and (c) two diodes switch.
8. Each signal **can be input** either with or without a routing bit.
9. Silicon **can block** high-energy X-rays.
10. These results demonstrate that our algorithm **can improve** the verification accuracy.
11. This voltage region **can be divided** into three parts at the voltages V_1 and V_2.
12. We **can obtain** a power efficiency of 28 GIPS/w at a voltage of 0.65 V.

as a result

[As a result]는 [because]의 역(逆)이다.

The vase fell.

ACTION RESULT

The vase broke.

The vase fell. **As a result**, it broke.

II

The vase broke **because** it fell.

GOOD EXAMPLES

○ A device was added to the holder to heat a wafer directly. **As a result**, wafers heat up very rapidly.

○ Small, wearable monitoring devices will enable the continuous checking of a person' s physical condition, and thus treatment in the early stages of any problem. **As a result**, the rates of geriatric and other diseases should decline.

실험, 테스트, 계산(計算) 등의 결과를 도입하는 경우, [as a result]를 쓰지 말 것.

TYPICAL MISTAKES

× *We evaluated a test chip. <u>As a result</u>, the new circuit consumed less power than a conventional one.*

- 새로운 회로(回路)의 전력 소비량이 적은 것은, 측정 되었기 때문이 아니라, 보다 나은 설계에 의한 것이다.

○ ... **The results showed that** the new circuit consumed less power ...

○ ... **We found that** the new circuit consumed less power ...

× *I-V measurements were made on mesa structures 200 μm in diameter. <u>As a result</u>, high resistivities above 5×10^7 Ωcm were obtained.*

○ I-V measurements were made on mesa structures 200 μm in diameter; and high resistivities above 5×10^7 Ωcm were obtained.

× *The crystal parameters were calculated from these indices. <u>As a result</u>, the lattice volume was larger for the new phase than for the parent phase.*

○ ... **It was found that** the lattice volume was larger ...

○ ... **The results showed that** the lattice volume was larger ...

is thought

POINT

[라고 여겨진다]를 그대로 [is thought]라고 번역하면, 대개의 경우 틀린 것이 된다.

DEFINITION: [Is thought]는, 어떤 분야의 사람들에게 공통(共通) 한 생각을 가리킨다. 즉, 그 생각은 일반적으로 인정되고 있는 것이다.

자기의 실험 결과 또는 개인의 의견을 말할 때, [Is thought]는 쓰지 않는다.

× *This slight difference is thought to be caused by the difference in size between the one-dimensional wires.*

- 이 기술(記述)은 연구자의 실험결과에 관한 것이다. 이 결과가 발표될 때까지 다른 사람은 몰랐기 때문에, 그것은 일반적으로 받아들여진 것이 아니다.

NOTE 한국어에서 「라고 여겨진다」란 표현은 어떤 발안(發案)이나 아이디어가 옳은 듯한 느낌이 짙은데에, 그것을 증명할 수 없을 적에 자주 쓰이고 있다. 영어에서는 이러한 케이스를 대개 [probably]를 써서 표현 할 수 있다. 그것이 적절치 않으면, [seem] 또는 다른 표현을 쓰면 된다.

~~is thought~~ →

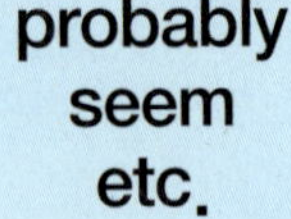

○ This slight difference is **probably** caused by the difference in ...

○ This slight difference **seems** to be caused by the difference in ...

○ This slight difference is **almost certainly** caused by the difference in ...

TYPICAL MISTAKES

× *In the degraded image, one row is completely black. <u>This is thought to be</u> due to a short circuit.*

○ ... **This is probably** due to a short circuit.

× *Since bubbles appeared after curing, this film <u>is thought to contain</u> a large amount of solvent.*

○ ... this film **probably contains** a large amount of solvent.

× *This film was deposited at 150℃, <u>which is thought to be</u> the optimum deposition temperature.*

○ ... 150℃, **which seems to be** the optimum deposition temperature.

GOOD EXAMPLES

NOTE 새로운 아이디어를 일반적으로 받아들여지는 생각과 대조적 시키는 경우, 먼저 [is thought]를 써서 일반적인 생각을 제시하고, 다음에, [but] 혹은 [however] 등으로 시작하는 문장으로 일반적인 생각과 다른 새로운 아이디어를 나타낸다.

○ **Generally, it is thought that** development proceeds through the dissolution of resist molecules decomposed by the e-beam. **However,** our result do not support that idea. We found that...

○ **Previously, it was thought that** annealing just caused the shrinkage and disappearance of small clusters to establish a local thermodynamic equilibrium. **But**...

○ **It was thought that** actually making a practical high-voltage electron gun required many technical advances. **However,** ...

becomes vs. is

POINT

[Becomes] 와 [is]의 사용법 문제의 하나는 두 변수(變數) 사이의 관계에 걸린 것이다.

변 화

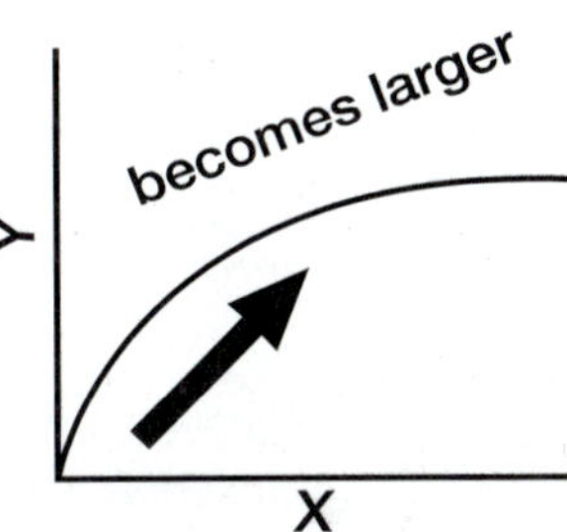

<u>변화의 표현</u>

- ○ Y becomes larger **as** X becomes larger.
- ○ Y increases **as** X increases.

[As]의 사용법에 주의

점

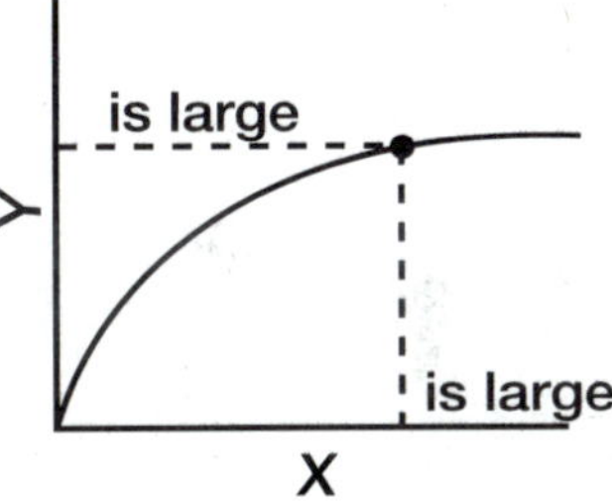

<u>점(点)의 표현</u>

- ○ Y is large **when** X is large.

NOTE [Becomes]와 [is]를 함께 사용하는 것은 보통 바람직 스럽지 않다.

- × *Y* **becomes** *large when X is large.*
- × *Y is large when/as X* **increases**.

ALSO NOTE:

- × *For these applications, it <u>becomes</u> important to reduce the temperature sensitivity.* (지금 중요치는 않지만, 언젠가 중요하게 된다는 의미인가?)
- ○ For these applications, it **is** important to reduce the temperature sensitivity. (지금 중요하다,)

TYPICAL MISTAKES

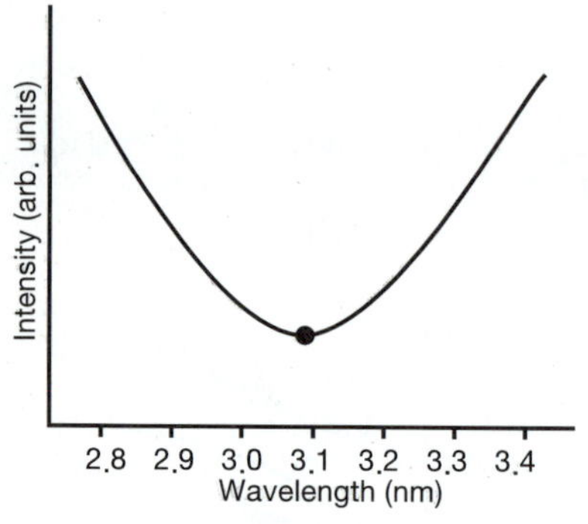

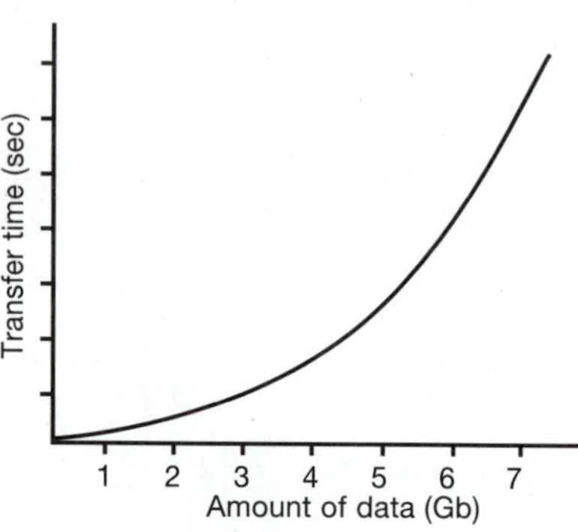

× *The intensity becomes a minimum when the wavelength is 3.1 nm.*

○ The intensity **is** a minimum **when** the wavelength **is** 3.1 nm.

○ The intensity **becomes** a minimum **as** the wavelength **approaches** 3.1 nm.

× *When the amount of data is large, the transfer time increases.*

○ **As** the amount of data **becomes** larger, the transfer time **increases**.

PRACTICE

다음 문장에 틀린 것이 있다. 틀린 것을 찾아내어 고쳐라.

PART A

1. The variation becomes worse as the voltage increases.
2. When V_{DD} is small, the delay increases.
3. If X is large enough, Z becomes negligible.
4. As X becomes stronger, Y increases.

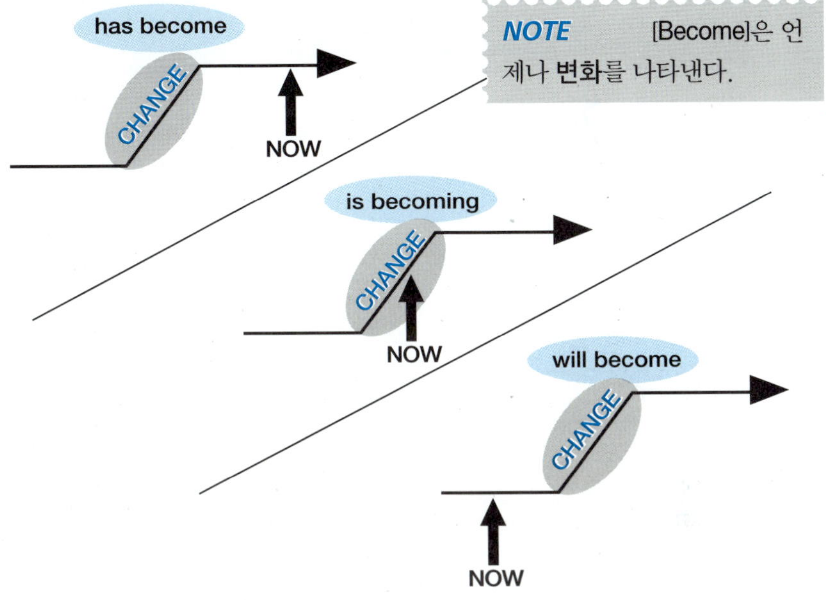

PART B

1. This process <u>has become</u> the conventional way of cleaning silicon wafers because of its excellent performance.
2. With this design, the gain of one stage <u>becomes</u> G_a/n, where G_a is the total gain of the amplifier and n is the number of stages.
3. The poor reliability of tungsten plugs <u>has already become</u> a serious problem in multilevel interconnections.
4. To track moving objects, it <u>becomes</u> necessary to match feature points in neighboring frames.
5. Resists of this kind <u>are becoming</u> increasingly important in deep submicron lithography.

remarkable

DEFINITION: Remarkable 한 것이란, 예외적 혹은 특별한 것이며, 사람들을 **깜짝놀라게** 하고 인상을 주는 것이다. [놀랄만한, 인상적인, 이상한, 예외적인, 드문] remarkably(부사)

기술(記述)영어에서 [remarkable]은 거의 쓰이지 않는다.

marked

DEFINITION: Marked 한 변화 또는 차이란, 매우 눈에띄는 명백한 변화 또는 차이이다. markedly(부사)

■ marked

- ○ There was **a marked increase** in the base current.
- ○ Above , there **is a marked reduction** in the efficiency.
- ○ We observed **a marked improvement** in the characteristics.
- ○ There are **marked differences** between the two devices.
- ○ The non-linearity **is more marked** for mind-size patterns.

■ markedly

- ○ As the growth temperature falls, the roughness **increases markedly**.
- ○ This design **markedly reduces** spherical aberration.
- ○ Annular illumination **does not markedly improve** the ultimate resolution.
- ○ The junction area of ultrathin-film SOI devices **is markedly smaller than** that of bulk ones.

NOTE [Marked] 대신에 다음 단어도 쓰인다.

observable noticeable significant pronounced

: Colon :

NOTE 콜론 앞에 스페이스를 넣지 말 것.

1. 열거(列擧)항목의 도입(導入)

There are three main sources of power consumption in digital CMOS circuits: switching power, short-circuit power, and leakage power.

Figure 1 shows the three types of inductors studied in this work: (a) no ground shield(NGS), (b) solid ground shield(SGS), and (c) patterned ground shield(PGS).

The PGS offers several benefits:

- Inductor behavior is independent of variations in substrate resistivity.
- Inductor behavior is easier to model.
- The large silicon area under the inductor ...

2. [As follows]의 뒤에는 반드시, 또는 [following]의 뒤에 자주 사용

The algorithm is as follows:

(1) Get error value, *E*.

(2) Rotate joint by +1° and render.

(3) Get new *E*.

This graph can be understood as follows: The Y-axis is the data bit rate, while the X-axis is the input data timing ...

The stress (σ) is related to the height (*H*) and width (W) of a line by the following equation:

$$\sigma = \frac{6\,\gamma\cos\theta}{D}\left(\frac{H}{W}\right)^2. \qquad (4)$$

3. 특성, 조건, 패러미터 등의 일람표(table)에 사용

WRONG

Sensitivity	:	100 mW/cm^2
Contrast	:	> 60

CORRECT

Sensitivity:	100mW/cm^2
Contrast:	> 60

OR

Sensitivity:	100 mW/cm^2
Contrast:	> 60

Unnecessary Repetition

대명사를 써서, 같은 단어의 반복을 피하라. 경우에 따라서는, 문장을 재구성 하도록 하자.

■ **BAD:** SiO_2 mask stripes are formed on a (100) n-InP substrate. The mask stripes are oriented parallel to the [011] direction. The spacing between the mask stripes is 2 μm.

■ **GOOD:** Sio_2 mask stripes are formed on a (100) n-InP substrate. **They** are oriented parallel to the [011] direction **and** have a spacing of 2 μm.

■ **BETTER:** SiO_2 mask stripes spaced 2 μm apart are formed on a (100) n-InP substrate parallel to the [011] direction.

PRACTICE

불필요한 반복을 없애라.

1. We paid special attention to the influence of the subband system, and to the possibility of observing the subband system at high temperatures.
2. The overcoat was about 0.1 μm thick. The overcoat was removed after baking.
3. This mesa structure is not easy to bury because the mesa structure has no mask on top.
4. This is an example of an action logic table. This action logic table can also be transformed into Prolog.
5. We developed a global router for high-speed bipolar LSIs. This global router minimizes areas ...
6. We observed the spots to estimate the amount of relaxation in the lattice parameters. The results of the observation of the spots revealed that the lattice parameters are relaxed in two steps.
7. This is the circuit we designed. The circuit was fabricated on a CMOS process.

Prepositions 3

빈칸을 적절한 전치사를 메꾸어라. 만일 필요 없으면, X로 메꾸어라.

REVIEW

a. X is equal ___________ Y.
b. X ha an effect ___________ Y.
c. This section explains ___________ the method.
d. Result X agrees ___________ result Y.
e. X is suitable ___________ Y.
f. X has an influence ___________ Y.
g. X causes ___________ Y.
h. X depends ___________ Y.
I. X is called ___________ Y.
j. X consists ___________ Y and Z.

CHECK YOUR KNOWLEDGE

1. X is responsible ___________ Y.
2. X is similar ___________ Y.
3. This paper concerns X.
4. ___________ the other hand, ...
5. a change ___________ the voltage
6. X is capable ___________ Y.
7. X is in good agreement ___________ Y.
8. X is different ___________ Y.
9. X is ___________ the order ___________ 10^6.
10. X corresponds ___________ Y.

Section 4

control

respectively

common vs. popular

recently

introduce

Adjective Formation (-ed)

Adjective Formation (-ing)

Punctuation: Comma 1

Style: Unnecessary Words 1

Prepositions 4

control

Ex. 1: 자동차의 핸들 조작(操作)을 생각해 보자. 핸들로 자동차의 움직이는 방향을 제어(制御0 한다. [제어한다]에는 두 가지 의미가 있다.

NO CHANGE	CHANGE

자동차를 직진시킬 경우, 핸들을 그대로 고정하고, 핸들을 꺽지 않는다.	자동차를 회전시킬 경우, 핸들을 꺽는다.

Ex. 2: 에어컨에 의한 실온제어(室溫制御)를 생각해 보자. 실온이 높은 경우, 에어컨은 온도를 바꾸어 방을 서늘하게 한다. 실온이 적절하면, 온도를 바꾸지 않는다.

NOTE [Control]이란 바라는 일을 하는 **능력을 발휘하는** 것을 가르킬 따름으로, 무언가가 실제로 **변화하고 있는 것을 의미하는 것이 아니다.** 변화시키고 싶지 않을 때는 그것을 유지 할 수가 있고, 변화시키고 싶을 때는 변화시킬 수가 있다.

control ≠change, adjust

TYPICAL MISTAKES

× *You make a car turn by controlling the steering wheel.*

○ You make a car turn by **turning** the steering wheel.

○ You **control the direction** in which a car moves by means of the steering wheel.

× *The lasing wavelength can be changed very rapidly by <u>controlling</u> the currents to the three electrodes.*

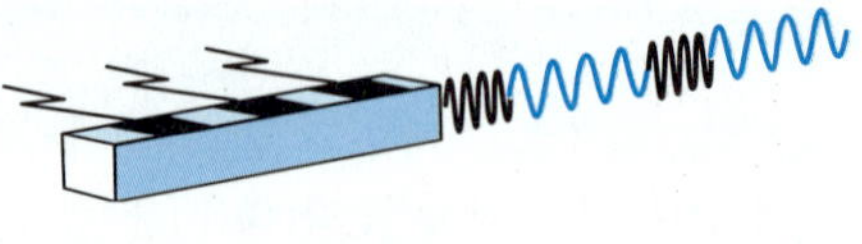

- 전류를 control 한다는 것은 전류를 변화시키거나 또는 일정치(一定値)를 유지시키는 능력을 발휘하는 것이며, 그것이 실제로 변화하고 있다는 의미가 아니기 때문에 이 문장은 무의미하다.

○ The lasing wavelength can be changed very rapidly by **adjusting/changing** the currents to the three electrodes.

○ The lasing **wavelength is controlled** by means of the currents to the three electrodes.

- 한국어에서는, 전류를 제어(制御)하여 파장(波長)을 변화시킨다고 쓰기도 하지만, 영어의 생각 방식은 역(逆)이다. 전류의 조정(調整)에 의해 파장을 control 한다. **즉, 일반적으로 [control]은, 구극(究極)의 목적 또는 바람의 결과에 관하여 쓰이고 있다.**

× *The roughness of the silicon surface needs to be <u>controlled</u> before oxidation.*

- 거치름을 control 한다는 것은, 반드시 거치름을 바꾼다는 의미가 아니다.

○ The roughness of the silicon surface needs to be reduced before oxidation.

NOTE 변수(變數)를 어느 치(値) 또는 두 치의 사이에 control 한다고 말하는 편이 적절치 않다. 이 경우, 그 변화를 **set** 하든가, **change** 하든가 **vary** 하는 것 처럼 설명하자.

× *The frequency can be <u>controlled from 9 to 11 GHz</u>.*

○ The frequency can be **varied between** 9 and 11 GHz.

○ The frequency can be **set to any value from** 9 to 11 GHz.

× *When the input power is large, the bias current is <u>controlled at a low level</u>.*

○ When the input power is large, the bias current is **set to** a low level.

○ When the input power is large, the bias current is **kept at** a low level.

respectively

POINT

영어의 [respectively]는 한국어의 [**각각**]과 완전히 같은 것이 아니다.

[Respectively]를 쓰는 데는 **두 리스트**가 필요하며 그 리스트의 각 항목(項目)은 엄밀히 **페어(pair)가 되어 있지 않으면 안 된다.**

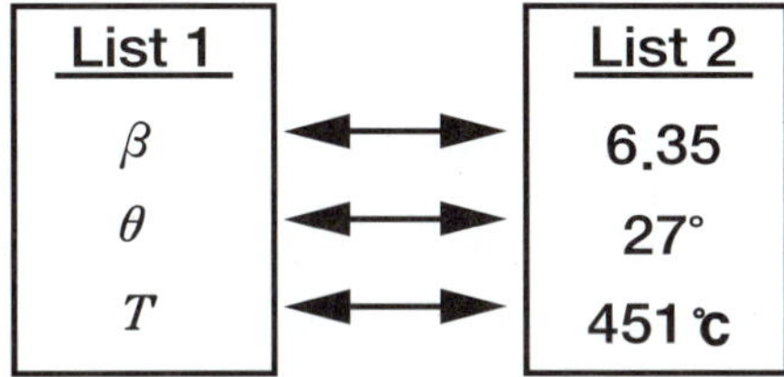

○ β, θ, and T have values of 6.35, 27°, and 451℃, respectively.

TYPICAL MISTAKES

Not a list!

× *The two amplifiers had input powers of -10 dBm and 6 dBm, respectively.*

- 이 문장은, 한국어로는 [각각]을 써도 좋지만, 영어에서는 [respectively]를 써서는 안 된다.

○ The two amplifiers had input powers of -10 dBm and 6 dBm.

○ Amplifier 1 and Amplifier 2 had input powers of -10dBm and 6dBm, respectively.

Not lists! Not lists!

× *The pulse widths were 13 ps for the pump and 5 ps for the signal, respectively.*

○ The pulse widths were 13 ps for the pump and 5 ps for the signal.

NOTE [Respectively]가 쓰이는 경우에도, 아래의 예처럼, 그것을 쓰지 않고 작문하면 역(逆)으로 한층 더 간단히 알기가 쉽고, 더욱 짧게 되는 경우도 있다.

OK: The threshold current and maximum output power are 1.5 mA and 70 mW, respectively.

BETTER: The threshold current is 1.5 mA, and the maximum output power is 70 mW.

PRACTICE

다음 문장에서 [respectively]가 올바르게 쓰이고 있는 문장을 골라라.

1. These graphs show Z versus X and Y, respectively.
2. This graph compares the sensitivity curves of three resists. The pKa values in water are -20, -6, and -2, respectively.
3. For gaps of 30, 20, 15, and 10 μm, the finest resolution is 90, 80, 70, and 60 nm, respectively.
4. The threshold current was 3.2 mA for a 15-μm-diameter mesa and 6.5 mA for a 25-μm-diameter mesa. The maximum output powers were 0.85 mW and 2 mW, respectively.
5. The conditions were an applied pressure ranging from 139 to 417 Pa, and a vacuum of 10 Torr, respectively.
6. The orange and blue lines are for devices 5 μm and 10 μm in diameter, respectively.
7. The exposure time is different for the first and second exposure, respectively.
8. Only an area with horizontal and vertical dimensions of 2.4 mm × 0.24 mm, respectively, can be illuminated.
9. We kept the RF power and the cleaning temperature at the optimum values of 220 W and 260℃, respectively.
10. The testing pads are placed on wires in the 1st, 2nd, and 3rd metal layers, respectively.
11. The static decision IC and the frequency divider IC cover operating ranges of 20 Gbit/s and 20 GHz, respectively.

common vs. popular

DEFINITION: 어떤 것이 common 하다는 것은 그것이 **자주 일어나는, 자주 있는**, 눈에 띄는, 흔하다는 의미이다.

Common, but not popular.

GOOD EXAMPLES

- Green tea is a common drink in Korea.
- Passwords and personal identification numbers are the most **common** methods of user authentication.
- Etching with a solution of H_2SO_4 and H_2O_2 is a very **common** cleaning technique.
- Communication networks are becoming more **common** in intelligent buildings in metropolitan areas.

DEFINITION: 어떤 것이 popular 하다는 것은 그것이 많은 사람들을 즐겁게 하며 **인기가 있다**는 의미이다.

Popular, but not common.

기술영어에서 [popular]는 거의 쓰이지 않는다.

GOOD EXAMPLES

- Green tea is a **popular** drink in Korea.
- Soccer is the most **popular** sport in Europe.
- Chocolate is always **popular** with children.

PRACTICE

적절하다고 여거지는 [common]이나 [popular], 또는 양쪽을 골라라.

1. Cellular phones are becoming very **common/popular** throughout the world.
2. Aluminum is a very **common/popular** material in silicon LSI fabrication.
3. Gucci is a very **common/popular** brand among young women.
4. Protocol LSIs and signal processing LSIs are very **common/popular** types of LSIs.
5. Beat Takeshi is a very **common/popular** TV personality.
   [TV personality = TV 탤런트]
6. Dogs are very **common/popular** pets in Korea.
7. This is one of the most **common/popular** methods of cleaning silicon for LSI fabrication.

recently

POINT

한국어의 「**최근(最近)**」이란 단어는 가까운 과거와 현재 양쪽이 포함되어 있는데 반하여, 영어의 [recently]는 가까운 과거만을 포함한다.

DEFINITION: Recently에 발생했다는 것은, 조금전 과거에 발생했다는 것이다.

[Recently]에 현재형은 쓰이지 않는다.

× *Recently, many such algorithms <u>are reported</u>.*

○ Recently, many such algorithms **have been reported**.

[Recently]는 과거를 가리키고 있다.

지금 일어나고 있는 것에 [recently]는 쓰이지 않는다.

× *<u>Recently</u>, portable battery-operated equipment <u>is</u> in widespread use.*

○ Portable battery-operated equipment **is now** in widespread use.

× *<u>Recently</u>, medium-sized nickel-metal hydride batteries <u>have been used</u> in hybrid cars in combination with a conventional engine.*

○ Medium-sized nickel-metal hydride batteries **are now being used** in hybrid cars in combination with a conventional engine.

PRACTICE

다음 문장에 [recently]는 올바르게 사용되어 있는가 아닌가 확인하라. 틀린 것이 있으면 고쳐라.

1. A big milestone (이정표 里程標) was recently reached when...
2. Recently, these systems are investigated ...
3. Recently, Dr. Sato asserted (단언 斷言)하다. that the cleaning solution used on production lines is not very clean.
4. Recently, the operating speed of CMOS LSIs reaches about 4 GHz.
5. We have recently moved to the new SR facility at our labs.
6. Recently, a great deal of attention is paid to these defects.
7. Recently, X-ray lithography was applied to the fabrication of this circuit in 2005.
8. Recently, the significance of this phenomenon has been pointed out.
9. Recently, portable equipment uses low-voltage LSIs.
10. Recently, this method has been widely used.

    주: 이 방법을 일반적(conventional) 이다.

11. Until recently, we were unable to clarify the origin of these defects.
12. Recently, several organizations have developed their own steppers.
13. Recently, it is becoming more important to reduce costs.

introduce

POINT

기술영어(技術英語)에서는 [introduce]는 자주 틀리게 쓰이고 있다.

× *To cook the food, we introduced a pan.*

NOTE 일상영어(日常英語)에서, 이 문장은 이상하게 틀린다. 기술영어에서는, 이 [introduce]의 쓰임새는 부자연스럽다.

○ To cook the food, we used a pan.

~~introduce~~  use/employ

× *In order to widen the output spectrum, we introduce an optical gate to suppress oscillations in the amplifier.*

○ ... we **use/employ** an optical gate to ...

× *To reduce the driving voltage, we <u>introduce</u> a push-pull drive configuration.*

○ ... we **use/employ** a push-pull drive configuration.

× We <u>introduced</u> cream to make the coffee taste better.

NOTE 앞의 예와 마찬가지로, 이 예문도 부자연스럽다.

○ We **added** cream to make the coffee taste better.

~~introduce~~  add

× *We <u>introduced</u> a small hole in the center of the defect cavity to change the resonant wavelength.*

○ We **added** a small hole ...

○ We made a small hole ...

× *We <u>introduced</u> battery protection circuits to prevent overcharging.*

○ We **added** battery protection circuits to prevent overcharging.

구두발표(口頭發表)의 경우 

 explain
describe

× *Next, I'll <u>introduce</u> to you the theoretical model of our single-electron device.*

○ Next, I'll **explain** the theoretical model of our single-electron device.

× *Next, I'll introduce the device structure.*

○ Next, I'll **explain/describe** the device structure.

× *First of all, I'll <u>introduce</u> our fully-depleted SOI MOSFETs.*

○ First of all, I'll **describe** our fully-depleted SOI MOSFETs.

올바른 사용법

[Introduce]의 쓰임새는 주로 두가지 있다. 기본적인 아이디어로서, 지금까지 없었던 것을 어느 환경에 새로이 도입(導入)하는 것이다.

어떤 기술(技術)을 처음으로 쓰는 경우

○ To build over-100-GHz millimeter-wave systems with practical components, we think that it will be necessary to **introduce** photonic technologies **into** electronic systems.

○ Discussions are continuing on how much further optical lithography can be extended and when it will be necessary to **introduce** the next-generation lithography.

무엇인가를 완전히 다른 타이프의 것에, 새로 삽입하는 경우

Ex. 1: 어떤 물질이나 화학성분을 어떤 장소에 가져가든가, 다른 물질에 도입한다.

○ It take 1.5 min. to **introduce** <u>the fluoro-compound</u> **into** <u>the chamber</u> and raise the pressure to 4 MPa.

○ One way to reduce the absorption at 13 nm is to **introduce** <u>aromatic rings into a polymer</u>.

Ex. 2: 오차(誤差)의 원인을 도입한다.

○ In extreme ultraviolet lithography (EUVL), the use of off-axis incident light for exposure **introduces** <u>a new source of pattern placement error</u> during printing.

Ex. 3: 재료에 장력(張力)을 준다.

○ This structure makes it unnecessary to **introduce** <u>strong strain</u> **into** <u>the active layer</u> to obtain polarization independence.

Adjective Formation (-ed)

명사 - 과거분사

A battery powers the system.

▼

The system is powered by a battery.

수동태(受動態)

a battery-powered system

NOTE 이 형식의 문장을 이해 하는데는 **역방향**으로 읽으면서, 하이픈 대신 적절한 **전치사**를 넣는다.

battery ← by ← powered ← system

Ex. 1: The mountain is covered with snow. → It is a snow-covered mountain.
Ex. 2: The engine is cooled by water. → It is a water-cooled engine.

PRACTICE

다음 문장을 완성하라.

PART A

1. The design is aided by a computer. What kind of design is it?
   It is ______________________________ .
2. The silicon is doped with boron. What kind of silicon is it?
   It is ______________________________ .
3. The pulse is generated by a laser. What kind of pulse is it?
   It is ______________________________ .

PART B

Ex: What is a battery-powered system?
It is a system that is powered by a battery.

1. What are hand-made shoes?
   They are ______________________________ .
2. What are semiconductor-based components?
   They are ______________________________ .
3. What is a speed-oriented circuit technique?
   It is ______________________________ .

Adjective Formation (-ing)

명사 - 현재분사

The diode emits light.

능동태(能動態)

a light-emitting diode

light ← emits ← diode

NOTE 이 형식의 문장을 이해하기 위해서는 **역방향(逆方向)**으로 읽으면 된다.

Ex. 1: The design saves energy.	→ It is an energy-saving design.
Ex. 2: The work consumes time.	→ It is time-consuming work.

PRACTICE

다음 문장을 완성하라.

PART A

1. The mechanism holds a wafer. What kind of mechanism is it?
   It is ______________________________ .
2. The copper contains zirconium. What kind of copper is it?
   It is ______________________________ .
3. The performance leads the industry. What kind of performance is it?
   It is ______________________________ .

PART B

Ex.: What is a light-emitting diode?
It is a diode that emits light.

1. What is dispersion-reducing fiber?
   It is ______________________________ .
2. What are noise-reducing techniques?
   They are ______________________________ .
3. What is wire-bonding equipment?
   It is ______________________________ .

PRACTICE

다음 질문에 답하라. 밑줄 그어진 단어가 주어가 아닌 경우, 먼저 문장을 수동태로 바꾸어 질문에 답하라.

Ex. 1: This appliance saves time. What kind of appliance is it?
It is a **time-saving** appliance.

Ex. 2: Oil fuels the power plant. What kind of power plant is it?
먼저, power plant를 주어로 한다.
The power plant is fueled by oil.
It is an **oil-fueled** power plant.

1. The resist is rinsed with water. What kind of resist is it?

   ______________________________.

2. The network switches packets. What kind of network is it?

   ______________________________.

3. The rice is fried in a pan. What kind of rice is ti?

   ______________________________.

4. A college educated the woman. What kind of woman is she?

   ______________________________.

5. This structure blocks the current. What kind of structure is it?

   ______________________________.

6. This equipment sorts letters. What kind of equipment is it?

   ______________________________.

7. The device was grown at a low temperature. What kind of device is it?

   ______________________________.

8. The user specifies the parameters. What kind of parameters are they?

   ______________________________.

9. This factor limits the rate (of the chemical reaction). What kind of factor is it?

   ______________________________.

, Comma 1 ,

1. 시작의 도입적(導入的) 또는 과도적(過渡的)인 표현

First, it is much easier to accurately measure ...

However, these experiments only provided ...

For uniaxial stress, several configurations are shown in Fig. 3.

2. 중간의 과도적인 표현

The ER spectrum, in fact, is more reminiscent of an atomic line spectrum...

3. 시작의 부사절

If the sample is properly conducting, the current can pass through it directly.

4. 리스트의 항목 가르기

The effect is sensitive to the resist thickness, bake parameters, adhesion, humidity, etc.

The key issues are defect detection, repair, and reduction.

NOTE 흔히, 리스트의 항목은 둘 이상 있으며 [and]앞에 콤마를 넣는다. 다음같은 예의 경우에는, 콤마는 불가결하다.

× *The materials used for the three layers were InGaAs, InGaAsP and InGaAs and InP.*

두 번째 레이어는 InGaAsP에 의해 되어 있는지, 아니면 InGaAsP와 InGaAs에 의해 되어 있는지 분명치 않다. 올바른 문장은 아래와 같다.

○ The materials used for the three layers were InGaAs, InGaAsP and InGaAs, and InP.

InGaAs
InGaAsP & InGaAs
InP

5. 기호의 도입

... the threshold voltage, V_{th}, ...

NOTE 이 경우 괄호를 써도 좋다.

... the threshold voltage (V_{th})...

단, 문장 전체가 같은 문체로 통일되어야 한다.

콤마는 기호의 도입에 언제나 쓴다고는 할 수 없다. 기호를 생략해도 문장이 성립 할 적엔, 콤마를 넣을 필요가 있다.

Ex. 1: Substrate effects degrade the quality factor, Q. [OK]
Q를 생략: Substrate effects degrade the quality factor. [OK]
두 번째 문장은 올바르기 때문에, 첫 번째 문장의 심볼 앞에 콤마가 필요하다.

Ex. 2: Consider a device of length L. [OK]
L을 생략: Consider a device of length. [No good]
두 번째 문장은 의미가 통하지 않으므로, 첫 번째 문장의 심볼 앞에 **콤마를 넣어서는 안 된다.**

PRACTICE

다음 문장에 콤마를 넣어라.

1. Also both designs use amplifiers.
2. As this model suggests holes can drift through the channel.
3. At 50 kV about half the electrons pass through the silicon membrane.
4. This provides an extra gate drive V_{kink} to the transistor.
5. Using multipass writing we have demonstrated 36-nm image placement.
6. Table 2 compares length area and execution times for each case.
7. When sufficient current is injected as the clock rises the voltage follows the clock.
8. Finally the spectra range in amplitude from 10^{-5} to as much as 10^{-2}.
9. Consider as an example an ASIMD chip with a SynchLink interface.
10. The top curve shows the reflectance R measured at room temperature.

Unnecessary Words 1

A dog is an animal.
다음과 같이 말할 수 있을까?
I have a dog animal.
답은 [노]이다. 누구든지 개가 무엇인지 알고 있으므로, [animal]이란 단어는 필요가 없다.

Reactive-ion etching is a technique.
자, 다음 문장을 음미해 보자.
The waveguide is formed by the reactive-ion-etching technique.
[Technique]이란 단어는 과연 필요할까? 먼저, 그것을 없애면 문장의 의미가 어떻게 바뀌는지 보자.
The waveguide is formed by reactive-ion etching.
의미는 전혀 변치 않는다. 즉, 여기서 [technique]란 단어는 **불필요**하다. 이러한 잘못은 한국어를 영어로 직역하는 경우에 자주 발생한다.
다음 단어들은, 표현의 뒤에 자주 첨가되는 영역불요(英譯不要)한 확률이 높은 것들이다.

effect, operation, process, technique

이러한 단어를 쓸 필요가 있는가 없는가를 판단하려면, 먼저 그것을 삭제 하여 의미가 변하는지 아닌지 테스트해 보는 것이다.

PRACTICE

밑줄 친 단어가 올바르게 쓰였는지 아닌지 검토해 보라.

1. The shielding effect provided by the 3D structure enables a variety of passive function devices to be fabricated.
2. To monolithically integrate the devices, we employ a regrowth technique.
3. ...the quantum-confined Stark effect comes into play.
4. Anisotropic Si etching technology is one of the most important

technologies for bulk micromachining processes.

5. The collimation effect is caused by the flaring of the potential boundary ...
6. One critical problem is short-channel effects, such as threshold voltage shift.
7. This structure is essential for achieving low-threshold-current, high-output-power operation.
8. ...an offset-canceling technique is employed in the limiting amplifier.
9. We use two special techniques for the fabrication: an image reversal process and a pattern-dependent oxidation process.
10. The high speed results from the suppression of the current blocking effect.
11. The interconnection lines are formed by lift-off and an air-bridge technique.
12. The p+regions are formed by Zn diffusion during the alloying process.
13. This device employs a Coulomb blockade effect to manipulate individual electrons.
14. The inverse square dependence suggests that Auger effects are involved.

Prepositions 4

빈칸을 적절한 전치사를 메꾸어라. 만일 필요 없으면, X로 메꾸어라.

REVIEW

a. X is responsible ____________ Y.
b. X is identical ____________ Y.
c. This paper concerns ____________ Y.
d. X is suitable ____________ Y.
e. ____________ the other hand, ...
f. X equals ____________ Y.
g. X is independent ____________ Y.
h. X is capable ____________ Y.
I. X is ___________ the order ____________ 10^6 .
j. X influences ____________ Y.

CHECK YOUR KNOWLEDGE

1. This paper is concerned ____________ X.
2. X is added ____________ Y.
3. X is related ____________ Y.
4. X takes Y ____________ account.
5. X is connected ____________ Y.
6. an increase ____________ the length
7. X is comparable ____________ Y.
8. There is no information ____________ Y.
9. X is sandwiched ____________ Y and Z.
10. Sato *et al*. mention ____________ two problems ...

Section 5

effective

has been used vs. is used

number of

by vs. with

Broken Connection

multi-

coincide

Punctuation: Comma 2

Style: Unnecessary Words 2

Prepositions 5

effective

DEFINITION: 어떤 수법(手法)이 effective 하다는 것은, 그 수법이 바라는 결과를 낳는다는 것을 뜻한다.

NOTE 어떤 수법이 effective 하다는 것은, **그 수법이 베스트라는 의미가 아니고**, 그 수법을 써서 바라는 결과를 얻을 수 있다는 것 만을 의미한다. 예를 들면, 담배에 불을 붙이는 경우, 성냥, 확대경 (날씨가 좋은 날) 또는 용접(容接) 토치 등이 쓰인다. 이러한 방법은, 장점과 결점이 있지만, 모두 effective 하다.

effective의 사용법

be effective

- So, we have found the tool to **be** quite **effective**.

be effective in ___ing

- The polishing is very **effective in** mark**ing** the surface flat.
- Our SSBL system is very **effective in** enhanc**ing** the resolution.

be an effective way to (do)

- A thin nitrogen-doped layer is **an effective way to** suppress boron diffusion.
- **One of the most effective ways to** lower the power consumption is to reduce the supply voltage.

be an effective method of (doing)

- **The most effective method of** improv**ing** the RF characteristics is to shorten the gate length.
- Sacrificial oxidation and annealing in hydrogen **are effective methods of** reduc**ing** the defect density.

[Effective]를 쓴 구문(構文)에 많은 잘못이 발견된다. 다음 구문은 **영어가 아니므로**, 주의하라.

be effective to
be effective for

× *This technique <u>is effective to</u> improve the performance.*

× *This technique <u>is effective for</u> improving the performance.*

○ This technique **is effective in** improving the performance.

○ This technique **is an effective way to** improve the performance.

effective vs. efficient

DEFINITION: 어떤 수법이 efficient 하다는 것은, 그 수법이 시간, 에너지, 원료(原料)등을 절약한다는 것을 의미한다. 즉 효율적임을 가리킨다.

자택(自宅)에서 역(驛)까지 가는데 가장 좋은 방법은 무엇인가?

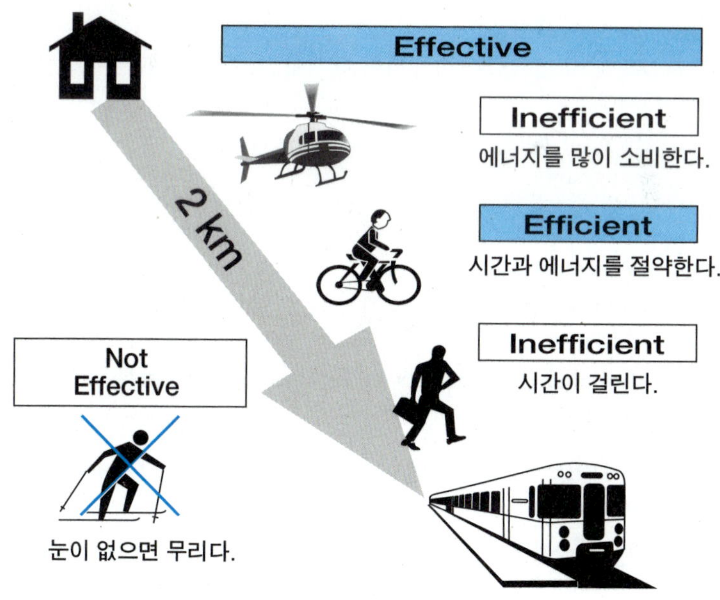

has been used vs. is used

POINT

[Has been used]는 현재가 아니고 과거를 가리킨다.

TYPICAL MISTAKES

× *In general, a voltage of 3.3 V <u>has been used</u> for I/O circuits.*

- 이 문장을 읽으면 3.3V의 전압은 지금까지 사용되었고, 앞으로는 다른 전압으로 바뀐다고 오해된다.

○ In general, a voltage of 3.3 V **is used** for I/O circuits.

- 일반적으로 3.3V의 전압이 사용되고 있다.

× *The chip set <u>has been used</u> in a cable television service and in a satellite television system.*

- 지금까지 이 칩세트가 사용되어 왔지만, 앞으로는 다른 것이 사용된다고 오해된다.

○ The chip set **is being used** in a cable television service and in a satellite television system.

× *In conventional CDR circuits, an external variable-delay line <u>has been used</u> to adjust the clock timing.*

- [Conventional]이란 말이 가리키는 것은, **일반적으로 사용되고 있는** 것이다. 즉 **현재**의 것이다.

○ In conventional CDR circuits, an external variable-delay line **is used** to adjust the clock timing.

× *The knife-edge method <u>has been used</u> to measure the diameter of an electron beam.*

○ The knife-edge method **is commonly used** to measure the diameter of an electron beam.

GOOD EXAMPLES

- **So far**, this system **has been used** to test more than 10 chips.
- Optical-fiber communication systems **have so far been used** mainly for high-speed, high-density, long-distance communications.
  - 이 문장은 장래 광통신 시스템이 다른 것에도 사용될 것임을 암시하고 있다.
- UHV scanning transmission microscopy (STM) **has been used for** the in-situ analysis of atomically flat GaAs surfaces. **However**, ex-situ atomic force microscopy(AFM) **is now** the method of choice for this kind of examination.
  - 이 문장은 지금껏 UHV STM 이 사용되어 왔지만, 현재는 ex-situ AFM이 선호되는 방법임을 의미한다.

PRACTICE

맞는 문장을 골라라. 또, 틀린것을 고쳐라.

1. Some of these ICs have already been used in 40-Gbit/s transmission experiments.
2. A lot of multimode fiber has been used for LANs in office buildings.
3. Three main methods have been used to grow crystals of organic materials.
4. Wavelength-division multiplexing systems are now being used in metropolitan and access networks.
5. The liquid crystal method has been used for hot-spot analysis for a long time, but now we need something better.
6. Recently, GaAs FETs have been widely used in circuits operating at microwave frequencies.
7. Organic solvents are widely used for the electrolyte of Li-ion batteries.
8. The amplifier we developed has been used in the transmitter and receiver of a 120-GHz-band wireless system.
9. Two types of power supply systems are used in telecommunications facilities.
10. Conventionally, lead-acid batteries have been used for backup power supplies.

number of

the number of Xs vs. the X number

The **number of rooms** is 9.

The **room number** is 201.

The **number of samples** is 5.

The **sample number** is 2.

TYPICAL MISTAKES

× *The <u>electrons' number</u> is about 100.*

○ The **number of electrons** is about 100.

× *As the <u>channel number</u> increases, integration becomes more difficult.*

○ As the **number of channels** increases, integration becomes more difficult.

× *For this chip, the total <u>gate number</u> is 780.*

○ For this chip, the total **number of gates** is 780.

○ For this chip, the total **gate count** is 780.

increase/reduce the number of

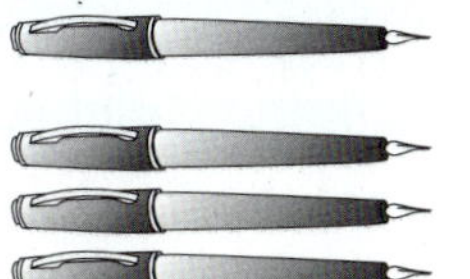

This is a pen. Can you reduce the pen?

These are pens. Can you reduce the pens?

어느 경우에 있어서도, 펜의 개념(概念) 자체는 수량(數量)을 갖고 있지 않기 때문에, 답은 [노]이다. 그러나 펜의 길이, 두께, 사이즈, 펜속의 잉크의 양등은 수량이 있기 때문에 그것들을 줄일 수 있다. 또, 물론 **펜의 수(數)도 줄일 수** 있다.

reduce the number of pens

사물(事物) 자체를 증감(增減) 할 수는 없다. 증감을 말하는 경우, 수량(數量) 등을 쓴다.

TYPICAL MISTAKES

× *The second point is how to reduce the terminals.*

○ The second point is how to **reduce the number of terminals**.

× *Use of the combined instruction reduced the steps in the procedure from 58 to 33.*

○ Use of the combined instruction **reduced the number of steps** in the procedure from 58 to 33.

× *The increase in the PL intensity is due to the decrease in the defects in the MQW.*

○ The increase in the PL intensity is due to **the decrease in the number of defects** in the MQW.

by vs. with

POINT

[로]의 번역 방식에 주의.

이 편지는 [펜]으로 씌었다. → This letter was written with a pen.

with + 구체적인 것

도구, **기구**(器具), **물체** 또는 **물질**을 써서 무언가를 하는 경우, [with]를 쓴다.

- The temperature was measured **with** a pyrometer.
- The substrates are rinsed **with** water.
- The surface was observed **with** a scanning electron microscope.

by + 추상적인 것

방법, **수순**(手順), **프로세스**, **테크닉** 등을 써서 무엇인가를 하는 경우, [by]를 자주 쓴다.

- The buffer layer was grown by molecular-beam epitaxy.
- The coordinates are calculated by simple addition.
- The gate patterns are extracted by procedure P1.
- The surface was observed by scanning electron microscopy.

NOTE [Make with]와 [fabricate with]는 **제조(製造) 프로세스**를 나타내는 데 쓰이는 경우도 있다. 이 사용법은 위의 논의(論議) 바깥에 있다.

- This part of the device must be fabricated **with** silicon technology.

다음 페어를 비교해서 그 차이를 음미하고, 문법의 면(面)에서 이해를 깊게 하라.

Describing what you do:

능동태: We generate the pulses with a fiber laser.

수동태: The pulses are generated **with** a fiber laser (by us).

Describing what happens:

능동태: A fiber laser generates the pulses.

수동태: The pulses are generated **by** a fiber laser.

PRACTICE

빈칸을 [by]나 [with]로 메꾸어라.

1. The surface morphology was observed ________ a microscope.
2. The pulses are encoded ________ a modulator.
3. They were fabricated ________ the following procedure.
4. This is the image produced ________ Sobel filtering.
5. It is difficult to control the wavelength ________ a conventional circuit.
6. During a measurement, we illuminate the region ________ a laser beam.
7. The zirconium is removed ________ an HF solution.
8. This chip was designed ________ the standard-cell method.
9. We form thin layers of WSi and Au ________ sputter deposition, and then make a Au side wall ________ electroplating.
10. The wafer is cleaved ________ an automatic cleaving machine.
11. We measured the performance ________ on-wafer probes.

Broken Connection

과거분사 + 전치사

다음 문장을 음미해 보자

○ The film is **deposited by ECR sputtering**.

여기서 이 필름이 광학적(光學的) 유용한 특성을 갖고 있음을 표현하려고 하나, 다음같이 말하는 것은 틀렸다.

× *Deposited film by ECR sputtering has useful optical properties.*

이 문장은 의미가 없다. 왜냐하면 [deposited]와 [by ECR sputtering] 사이의 관련(關聯)이 끊겨 있기 때문이다. 올바른 문장은 다음과 같다.

○ Film **deposited by ECR sputtering** has useful optical properties.
= Film (that is) deposited by ECR sputtering has ...

× *This effect becomes stronger as the number of coupled quantum dots to the quantum wire increases.*

○ This effect becomes stronger as the number of quantum dots coupled to the quantum wire increases.

method of

다음의 올바른 문장을 음미해 보자.

○ the **fabrication of** DFB **lasers**

[Fabrication] 뒤에 [method]란 단어를 넣으면 다음과 같이 된다.

× *the fabrication method of DFB lasers*

이 경우, 이 표현의 기본적 구조는 [method of lasers]로 되는 것에 주의 하라. 레이저는 수법(手法)을 갖고 있지 않으므로 위 문장은 의미가 성립되지 않는다. [Method]를 삽입함으로써 [fabrication]과 [of DFB lasers] 와의 사이의 관련이 잘려 버렸다. 올바른 표현은 다음과 같다.

○ a method of **fabricating DFB lasers**

○ a fabrication method **for** DFB lasers

× *An effective protection method against shocks during fabrication is also necessary.*

○ An effective method of **protecting against shocks** during fabrication is also necessary.

similar to

[Similar]뒤에 [to]를 쓰는 경우, 그 사이에 다른 단어를 넣지 말것.

× *Material A has a similar X-ray diffraction pattern to that of Material B.*

○ Material A has an X-ray diffraction pattern **similar to** that of Material B.

PRACTICE

관련(關聯)이 잘린 다음 표현을 고쳐라.

1. an estimation method of the current

   ____

2. Infrared spectroscopy produced similar results to those of the UV absorption analysis.

   ____

3. the waveform of transmitted signals over our new microstrip line

   ____

4. We have developed a new trimming technique of planar lightwave circuits.

   ____

5. Stored data is destroyed at a voltage of 1.8 V in a 1-V SRAM.

   ____

6. to develop a design method of DC electric-power-supply networks

   ____

7. an integration technique of transistors and photodiodes

   ____

8. Our interferometer is very small, but it provides a similar performance to that of a desktop mode.

   ____

9. The applied bias voltage to the device was −1.0 V.

   ____

multi-

[Multi-]는 접두어로 독립된 단어가 아니다

× *This device has <u>multi</u> electrodes.*

- [Multi]는 단어가 아니기 때문에, 형용사로서 쓰이지 않는다. 이 경우 [multiple]을 써야 한다.

○ This device has **multiple** electrodes.

[Multi-]로 시작하는 단어는, 다음 것을 빼면, 모두 다 형용사 이다.

× *This device has <u>multi-electrodes</u>.*

- [Multi-electrode]는 형용사이므로, 주어 같은 목적어로서 쓰이지 않는다. 또 그 복수형(複數形)도 존재하지 않는다.

○ This is a **multi-electrode device**.

명사: multimedia, multifoil, multimillionaire, multinomial, multiplet, multiplication, multiplier, multiplicand, multiplicity, multitude, multiversity

동사: multiply

[Multi-]뒤의 문자(文字)가 모음이고, 또 하이픈 삽입에 의해 단어의 발음이 알기쉬워질 경우, 하이픈을 삽입하라.

NO HYPHEN: multilevel, multistage, multiaddress
HYPHEN: multi-electrode

[Multi-]는 명사 또는 형용사와 결합할 수가 있다. 사전에서 그 올바른 형(形)을 체크하자.

multi- + 명사: multiaddress, multilane, multilevel, multistage
multi- + 형용사: multicolored, multicultural, multidirectional, multilateral, multinational

PRACTICE

다음 문장을 완성하라.

> Examples:
>
> What kind of device has several electrodes?
>
> A multi-electrode device does.

1. What kind of receiver has several channels?

   A ________________________________ does.

2. What kind of module holds several chips?

   A ________________________________ does.

3. What kind of circuit can perform many functions?

   A ________________________________ does.

4. What kind of structure has several layers?

   A ________________________________ does.

5. What kind of system has several processors?

   A ________________________________ does.

coincide

POINT

두 개의 사물(事物)이 coincide 한다는 것은, 그것들이 **같은 것이라는 것이 아니다.**

DEFINITION:

1. 어떤 이벤트가 다른 이벤트와 coincide 한다는 것은, 이 두 이벤트가 **동시에 일어남**을 가리킨다.
2. 두 사물이 coincide 한다는 것은, 이 두사물이 동시에 **같은 공간을 점(占)하고 있음**을 가리킨다.

The sharp drop in Y coincides with the rapid rise in A.

NOTE 횡축(横軸)은 시간이다.

이 단어는 위와 같은 특별한 의미를 지니기 때문에, 기술영어에서는 쓰는 경우가 적다.

→

agree with
be in good agreement with
equal
be (about) the same as

TYPICAL MISTAKES

× *These results coincide with those results.*

○ These results **agree with** those results.

× *It was found that the measured value coincided perfectly with the calculated one.*

○ It was found that the measured value **was in perfect agreement with (was exactly the same as)** the calculated one.

× *This result coincides with Gaussian beam theory.*

○ This result **agrees with** Gaussian beam theory.

× *This temperature coincides well with that derived from the curve in Fig. 5.*

○ This temperature **is about the same as** that derived from the curve in Fig. 5.

, Comma 2 ,

6. 두 긴 절(節)의 분할(分割)

Strong exciton features are seen at both E_0 and $E_0 + D_0$ transitions, and the E_2 peak is shown to consist of a number of closely spaced structures.

7. 코멘트의 절(節)이나 구(句)의 분할(分割)

The resist system and e-beam system, including proximity corrections, all affect the ability to build masks with tight image-size control.

Two identical amplifiers, one clocked off the rising edge and one clocked off the falling edge of the clock, are used to sample one data pin...

The fastest design was a two-stage shift register, which operated at clock frequencies of up to 250 MHz.

NOTE 형용사절을 써서 무엇인가를 명확히 하는 경우, 콤마는 삽입하지 않는다. that vs. which 항목(Section 2)를 참조 할것, 예를 들면

Only those chips **that passed the preliminary test** were used.

8. 문장의 뒤에 붙인 절(節)이나 구(句)의 분할(分割)

Only RTDs and Schottky diodes are used as circuit elements, greatly simplifying the fabrication process.

Microprocessor speeds continue to increase dramatically, with I/O and memory bandwidths becoming a limiting factor in system performance.

Three common electric-field modulation configurations are shown in Fig. 4, divided into "longitudinal" and "transverse" categories.

9. For example의 전후(前後)

In many iterative algorithms, for example, a SIMD array operates with massive parallelism for just a short time.

10. 수식(數式)과 뒤의 where 와의 사이

In this approximation, the rate equation for the reaction is

$$d[Xe^{n+}]/dt = k_{n+1}[Xe^{(n+1)+}] - kn[Xe^{n+}],$$

where k_n is the rate constant for the reaction.

PRACTICE

다음 문장에 콤마를 넣어라. 밑줄 친 부분은 주절(主節) 또는 주절의 중심 부분이다.

1. On the other hand if X is low Y will be low after the clock goes high.
2. These points are illustrated in Fig. 1 which compares three types of spectra for a typical semiconductor GaAs.
3. As shown in Fig. 2 the sample is extrinsically modulated by a source at some frequency *f*.
4. High voltage reduces scattering resulting in better resolution straighter side walls and reduced proximity effects.
5. With image placement targets as low as 35 nm all contributions must be minimized including those from the e-beam system and process-induced distortion.
6. However if these constraints are present problems arise if one attempts to simplify the timing graph.
7. In the transmission mode the spectrum is the relative change in transmittance $\Delta T/T$.
8. When the clock input is low transistors P3 and P4 act as resistive loads for the first stage which acts as a linear amplifier for small input swings and as a swing-limiter for large input swings.
9. Common digital layout procedures such as symbolic layout and layout compaction destroy the symmetry of critical analog layouts impacting performance.
10. All cases used 0.75--thick PMMA resist with the results being an average for isolated lines isolated spaces and equal-line/space arrays.
11. To maintain quasi-neutrality the electron concentration must be increased resulting in reduced source resistance.
12. In this model holes drift into the low-field source-gate region where they diffuse and recombine.

Unnecessary Words 2

[Is used to] 와 [observe]는 여분(餘分)이 되어 있는 경우가 적지 않다. 다음 페어(pair)인 문장을 음미해 보자.

A computer is used to control the movable mirrors.
A computer controls the movable mirrors.

As shown in these characteristics, bistability was observed.
These characteristics exhibit bistability.

어느 경우에도, 두 번째 구문(構文) 쪽이 심플하고 훨씬 더 좋다.

PRACTICE

PART A: 불필요한 [is used to]를 삭제하라.

1. The first test was used to clarify the degradation modes.

   ____

2. Optical fibers are used to transport light to and from the probe.

   ____

3. A Teflon lens was used to focus the signal on the detector.

   ____

4. This terraced structure is used to improve the heat dissipation of the chip.

   ____

5. An electro-optic probe was used to detect reflected and transmitted signals.

   ____

6. The tungsten is used to reduce the resistance of the source, drain, and gate.

   ____

PART B: 불필요한 [observed]를 삭제하라.

Examples:

Asymmetrical profiles are not observed.	→	There are no asymmetrical profiles.
New roughness generated through etching cannot be observed.	→	Etching generates no new roughness.

1. With optical fiber, a small power penalty is observed.

 ____

2. A similar spectrum was observed down to an input power of –5dBm.

 ____

3. Without an RF bias, a definite peak at 1.4 Å is observed.

 ____

4. No peak shift is observed either with or without an RF bias.

 ____

5. The edge of the pattern is distorted, and a vertical side wall cannot be observed.

 ____

6. Clear, well-defined eye openings were observed.

 ____

Prepositions 5

빈칸을 적절한 전치사로 메꾸어라. 만일 필요하다면 X로 메꾸어라.

REVIEW

a. X is composed __________ Y and Z.
b. X is equal __________ Y
c. X corresponds __________ Y
d. Result X agrees __________ result Y.
e. X is sandwiched __________ Y and Z.
f. X is related __________ Y
g. X takes Y __________ account.
h. a change __________ the voltage
I. X is in good agreement __________ Y
j. X is connected __________ Y

CHECK YOUR KNOWLEDGE

1. X is associated __________ Y
2. X gives rise __________ Y
3. X is superior __________ Y
4. As a result __________ X, ...
5. a decrease __________ the rate
6. There is a great deal of data __________ Y
7. X is suited __________ Y
8. X is characteristic __________ Y
9. fluctuations __________ the temperature
10. __________ contrast, ...

Section 6

then

one of the → a/an

depend on, consist of

Meaningless -ing

obvious

operating principle

most vs. most of

issue

so-called

therefore vs. so

Punctuation: Semicolon

Prepositions 6

then

POINT

기술영어에서는 [then]은 주로 다음 두 가지 의미로 쓰이고 있다.

행동의 순번(順番): First ... Next ... Then ...

○ **First**, the sample was rinsed. **Next**, it was put in the dryer chamber. **Then**, the chamber was heated.

○ The voltage was scanned up to −2.1 volts, and **then** back down.

○ Each bit is reshaped, and **then** stored temporarily in an output buffer.

조건문: If ..., (then) ...

NOTE NOTE: [If] 부분이 짧은 경우, [then]을 자주 생략한다.

○ If there is a fault here, (**then**) this circuit will never be reset.

○ If we set the failure criterion to be a drop of 10dB, **then** we estimate the lifetime of these devices to be over 100,000 hours.

○ If the width of the opening is much smaller than its depth, (**then**) it is difficult to fill the opening completely with metal.

TYPICAL MISTAKES

then ≠ 이므로, 그래서

× *A larger area means more expensive chips. <u>Then</u>, we have to limit this increase in area when we apply our technique.*

○ A larger area means more expensive chips. **So**, we have to limit ...

× *This increases the refractive index: <u>Then</u> the wavelength becomes longer.*

○ This increases the refractive index; **so** the wavelength becomes longer.

○ This increases the refractive index, **which makes** the wavelength longer.

× *The slopes of these lines are almost the same. <u>Then</u>, the failure modes are probably the same.*

○ The slopes of these lines are almost the same. **So**, the failure modes...

○ The slopes of these lines are almost the same. **That means that** the failure modes ...

one of the → a/an

POINT

일반적으로 [...의 하나]와 [a]나 [an]으로 번역하는 것이 가장 좋다.

다음 틀린 예문(例文)을 확인하자.

× *A dog is <u>one of the</u> animals.*

× *A dog is <u>one of the</u> kinds of animals.*

올바른 구문(構文)은 다음과 같고, 훨씬 간단하다.

○ A dog is **an** animal.

○ A dog is **a** kind of animal.

한편, [one of the] 라는 표현은, 다음 예처럼 자주 최상급의 형용사와 함께 쓰인다.

○ A tiger is **one of the dangerous** animals.

○ Aspirin is **one of the most effective** medicines for headaches.

One of the 라는 표현의 쓰임새를 음미해 보자.

TYPICAL MISTAKES

× *Although area bump technology is <u>one of the</u> solutions, it has ...*

○ Although area bump technology is **a** solution, it has ...

× *In such circuits, V_P is <u>one of the</u> crucial parameters.*

○ In such circuits, V_P is **a** crucial parameter.

× *Making wires narrower is <u>one of the</u> effective ways to reduce ...*

○ Making wires narrower is an effective way to reduce ...

○ Making wires narrower is **one of the most effective** ways to reduce...

× *Differential drive is <u>one of the</u> common designs for bipolar circuits.*

○ Differential drive is **a** common design for bipolar circuits.

○ Differential drive is **one of the most common** designs for bipolar circuits.

depend on, consist of

POINT

[Is depend on] 와 [is consist(ed) of]는 영어가 아니다.

~~is depend on~~  depends on

TYPICAL MISTAKES

× *The wavelength is depend on temperature.*

○ The wavelength **depends on** temperature.

× *The line-edge roughness should be depend on the size of the polymer aggregates.*

○ The line-edge roughness **should depend on** the size of the polymer aggregates.

~~is consist of~~
~~is consisted of~~  consists of

TYPICAL MISTAKES

× *This battery pack is consisted of two parallel sets of 15 cells in series.*

○ This battery pack **consists of** two parallel sets of 15 cells in series.

× *Our optical interconnections was consisted of SiO_2 and polymer.*

○ Our optical interconnections **consist of** SiO_2 and polymer.

× *A conventional target for resonant transition radiation (RTR) has been consisted of thin foils separated by vacuum.*

○ A conventional target for resonant transition radiation (RTR) **consists of** thin foils separated by vacuum.

Meaningless -ing

POINT

현재분사 (-ing) 구(句)의 주어는, 메인 동사의 주어와 같지 않으면 안 된다. 주어가 동일하지 않는 잘못은 현수분사(懸垂分詞) (dangling participle) 라고 한다. 영어를 모국어로 하는 사람도 이 잘못을 자주 범한다.

× *After eating lunch, an e-mail arrived.*

[Eating]의 주어가 [an e-mail]로 되어 있으므로, 이 문장은 다음과 같은 의미가 되어 버린다.

× *After an en-mail are lunch, it arrived.*

올바른 문장은 다음과 같다.

○ After **eating** lunch, **I** received an e-mail.

○ After lunch, an e-mail arrived.

TYPICAL MISTAKES

× *After depositing SiO_2, an area for the gate is opened by etching.*

○ After SiO_2 **is deposited**, an area for the gate...

○ After the **deposition** of SiO_2, an area for the gate ...

NOTE 기술영어에서, 이 문제는 대개 수동태 또는 명사를 써서 간단히 해결할 수 있으나, 때로는 완전히 고쳐 쓰지 않으면 안 되는 일도 있다.

× *After shortening the annealing time, the blue shift disappeared.*

○ When the annealing time **was shortened**, the blue shift disappeared.

○ Shortening the annealing time **caused** the blue shift to disappear.

× *Analyzing the results, there are two patterns.*

○ When the results **were analyzed**, two patterns were found.

○ An analysis of the results **revealed** two patterns.

× *Combining these functions, various types of processing can be performed.*

○ When these functions **are combined**, various types of ...

○ Through a **combination** of these functions, various types of ...

NOTE [Generally speaking], [strictly speaking], [judging from], [considering] 및 [supposing] 등의 숙어는 이것과는 관련이 없다.

obvious

POINT

[obvious]는 자주 독자에게 실례(失禮)하는 인상을 준다.

DEFINITION: 무엇인가가 obvious 하다는 것은, 매우 쉽사리 이해 할 수 있다는 것이다. 즉, 바보라도 이해할 수 있을 만큼 명백하다.

~~It is obvious that~~  (Nothing) / It is clear that

× *<u>It is obvious that</u> the oxygen-deficient atmosphere produced a polycrystalline film.*

○ The oxygen-deficient atmosphere produced a polycrystalline film.

○ **It is clear that** the oxygen-deficient atmosphere produced a polycrystalline film.

× *<u>It is obvious</u> from the graph <u>that</u> the pitch of interconnections is limited by the current density of via plugs.*

○ **It is clear** from the graph **that** the pitch of interconnections is limited by the current density of via plugs.

○ The graph **shows that** the pitch of interconnections is limited by the current density of via plugs.

clear
pronounced
prominent
observable, etc.

× *In this spectrum, the Si 2p peak is <u>obvious</u>.*

○ In this spectrum, the Si 2p peak is **quite prominent/pronounced**.

× *Every data pulse is demultiplexed without any <u>obvious</u> cross talk.*

○ Every data pulse is demultiplexed without any **observable/apparent** cross talk.

Obvious란 단어를 쓸 적에 특히 주의를 하자.
이 단어는 기술영어에서는 별로 쓰지 않는다.

operating principle

POINT

일반적으로 명사앞에 [operation]은 쓰지 않는다. 그 대신에 [operating]을 쓰자.

~~operation principle~~  operating principle

× *Figure 2 illustrates the <u>operation principle</u> of a 7th-order harmonic ring oscillator circuit.*

○ Figure 2 illustrates the operating principle of a 7th-order harmonic ring oscillator circuit.

NOTE [Principle of operation] 도 옳다.

~~operation~~ + 명사  operating +명사

× *One problem with an electro-optic switch is that the performance of the driver amplifier limits the <u>operation speed</u>.*

○ ...limits the **operating speed**.

× *Figure 7 shows the transient response of the circuit when the <u>operation mode</u> changes from precharge to evaluation.*

○ ... when the **operating mode** changes ...

× *For practical use, the equipment must function within the required <u>operation temperature</u> range.*

○ ... the required **operating-temperature** range ...

× *On-wafer measurements revealed the maximum <u>operation frequency</u> to be 39 GHz.*

○ ... the maximum **operating frequency** ...

× *To further expand optical communication networks, it is important to reduce <u>operation costs</u>.*

○ ... it is important to reduce **operating costs**.

most vs. most of

most 어떤 종류의 사물의 전부에 관해 일반적으로 말할 때 [most]를 쓴다.

Most apples are red.

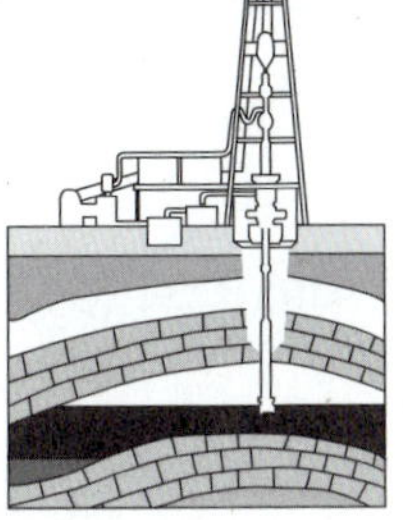

Most oil is deep underground.

× *Most of optical receivers have been designed for continuous signals.*

○ **Most** optical receivers have been designed for continuous signals.

× *Most of the semiconductor mode-locked lasers have a linear cavity.*

○ **Most** semiconductor mode-locked lasers have a linear cavity.

most of (the ...) 어느 **특정(特定)한 그룹이나 사물**에 관하여 말할 때 [**most of**]를 쓴다.

Most of the apples in the box are yellow. 특정한 그룹

Most of the oil imported into Korea comes from the Middle East. 특정한 것

× Most of peripheral functions of the power supply card are handled by a microcontroller.

○ **Most of** the peripheral functions of the power supply card are handled by a microcontroller.

× Most of flammable material in a Li-ion battery can be eliminated by using a nonflammable, nonvolatile electrolyte.

○ **Most of** the flammable material in a Li-ion battery can be eliminated by using a nonflammable, nonvolatile electrolyte.

다음 페어의 쓰임새는 [most]와 [most of]의 쓰임새와 거의 같다.

all ↔ all of

some ↔ some of

any ↔ any of

no ↔ none of

NOT ENGLISH!

× *Almost DC networks contain a DC-DC converter.*

○ **Most** DC networks contain a DC-DC converter.

○ **Almost all** DC networks contain a DC-DC converter.

× *Almost of sodium in the precursor was replaced with lithium.*

○ **Most of** the sodium in the precursor was replaced with lithium.

○ **Almost all of** the sodium in the precursor was replaced with lithium.

PRACTICE

다음 문장에서 올바른 것을 고르고, 틀린 것을 고쳐라.

1. Most diodes we fabricated contained one defect or none at all.
2. Most nanodevices are fabricated by EB lithography.
3. For the experiments, we chose a system that was smaller and simpler than most actual systems.
4. Most of the reported ring lasers have a high threshold current.
5. This fingerprint sensor can capture a clear image of most of the fingerprints.
6. Most carbon dioxide in the chamber remains liquid.
7. Most of the fabricated modules had a responsivity of more than 0.8 A/W.
8. Most beryllium atoms remain in the InGaAs layer.

issue

POINT

[Issue]는 해결해야 하는 또는 주목해야 하는 것이 아니라, 논의(論議)해야 (머리에 두어야 할) 일이다.

[Issue]는 사람들이 논하고 있는 중요한 토픽이다. 테크니컬 페이퍼에서 자주 논하는 토픽 또는 문제점을 언급할 때, [issue]를 쓴다.

discuss

○ Suppressing the leakage current is **the main issue** in the fabrication of ultralow-voltage LSIs.
  • 많은 연구자는 이방법에 관해 논하고 있다.

○ In this type of network, wavelength managements is **the key issue**.

○ **Another big issue** is the bandwidth limitation imposed by the electrical interface.

디자인, 공작(工作), 실험 등을 행할 때, 검토하지 않으면 안 될 요소(要素)를 나타낼 때는 [consideration]을 쓴다.

○ The temperature at which a Si nanowire is oxidized is **a very important consideration** in making SETs that operate at room temperature.

○ **An important consideration** is how precisely the optical subassembly can be put together.

○ The thermal stability of the sheet resistance is **an important consideration** in wafer selection and FET fabrication.

[Problem] 이란, 해결을 필요로 하는 일을 가르킨다.

solve

PROBLEM

○ **The remaining problem** is the large coupling loss between the waveguide and a fiber.

○ **One problem** with this type of switch is that the performance of the driver amplifier limits the operating speed.

○ However, **there is a problem with** the conventional template-matching method.

○ **Another problem** is how to control and stabilize the wavelength when the wavelength is switched.

Examples of issues and problems

Issue	Problem
cost	the high cost of the device
health & safety	the use of toxic chemicals for fabrication
yield	low yield
wavelength stability	how to reduce temperature fluctuations

PRACTICE

[Issue]나 [problem]을 다음 빈칸에 넣어라.

1. Dirt on the sensor surface is a serious _______ for fingerprint sensors.
2. One _______ is the stability of the transmission wavelength.
3. Cost performance is always an __________ because the construction of multichip modules involves many costly techniques.
4. One _________ with a dielectric filter is that the transmission wavelength depends on temperature.
5. To solve the phase fluctuation ________ , we developed a planar lightwave circuit.
6. User authentication to prevent the unauthorized use of equipment has become an important _______ .
7. The use of stabilization circuits is a good way to solve this _______ .
8. The mounting of optical devices, such as laser diodes, is an important _________ .
9. The final section discusses a(n) ________ that will soon become important in the photonic measurement of microwaves: integration and packaging technology.
10. The design _______ is how to achieve high-speed gain control.
11. The main __________ in extreme-ultraviolet lithography (EUVL) is the production of defect-free masks.

so-called

DEFINITION: [So-called]는, 틀렸거나, 오해를 불러 일으킬 염려가 있는 단어를 도입하는데 자주 쓰인다.

GOOD EXAMPLES

○ Sai Baba is a **so-called** "guru" with many followers.
- Guru는 정신적 리더이지만, Sai Baba는 단자 마술사이며 종교지도자는 아니다.

기술영어에서는 [so-called]는 거의 쓰이지 않는다.

(Nothing)
what is called
what [we] call

TYPICAL MISTAKES

× *This configuration produces a <u>so-called</u> off-axis Fourier hologram.*
○ This configuration produces an off-axis Fourier hologram.
○ This configuration produces **what is called** an off-axis Fourier hologram.
- 독자에게, 어떤 전문용어가 낯익지 않다고 여기는 경우, 그것을 소개하는데 [what is called]를 쓴다.

× *The MIT group suggested the <u>so-called</u> barrier-induced hole pile-up model.*
○ The MIT group suggested the barrier-induced hole pile-up model.
○ The MIT group suggested **what they call** the barrier-induced hole pile-up model.
- 어떤 전문용어는 누군가가 만든 것을 나타내는데 [what (they) call]을 쓴다.

× *Yamaguchi and his group developed the <u>so-called</u> chip-size-cavity package.*
○ Yamaguchi and his group developed the chip-size-cavity package.
○ Yamaguchi and his group developed **what they call** a chip-size-cavity package.

therefore vs. so

A = B and B = C.
Therefore,
A = C.

The computer is broken. So, we cannot use it.

DEFINITION: [Therefore]를 써서 논리적 결과나 결론을 이끈다.

DEFINITION: [So]를 써서 그 앞에 설명한 것의 경과(經過)를 말한다.

[Therefore]를 쓰는 장면은 적다.

so,
thus,
as a result,
etc.

TYPICAL MISTAKES

× *A networked control system (NCS) has many advantages: quick and easy maintenance, low cost, great flexibility, etc. Therefore, NCSs are increasingly being used for industrial control in a variety of fields.*

○ A networked control system (NCS) has many advantages: quick and easy maintenance, low cost, great flexibility, etc. **So**, NCSs are increasingly being used for industrial control in a variety of fields. (.. **This is why** NCSs are increasingly being used...)

× *The phosphorus distribution of WSiN films varies with thickness. Therefore, we investigated the dependence of thickness on the nitridation conditions.*

○ The phosphorus distribution of WSiN films varies with thickness. **So**, we investigated the dependence of thickness on the nitridation conditions. (...**This prompted us to investigate** the dependence....)

× *These systems use fixed-wavelength lasers, and component vendors must now stock many lasers for each wavelength in case of trouble. Therefore, inventory costs can be considerably reduced if a widely tunable laser is used as a replacement part.*

○ These systems use fixed-wavelength lasers, and component vendors must now stock many lasers for each wavelength in case of trouble. **So**, inventory costs can be considerably reduced if a widely tunable laser is used as a replacement part.

GOOD EXAMPLES

- 반응에 주어지는 가능성 있는 물질은 (1) 산소, (2) 오존, 둘 중 어느 것인지 알고 있다. 실험 결과 (1)은 부정(否定) 되었다.

○ These results eliminate oxygen as a possible reactant. **Therefore**, the initial stage of the reaction must involve ozone.

○ The maximum radiated power is 140 μW for each antenna element. **Therefore**, the maximum radiated power for the antenna array (9 elements) is about 1 mW.

- 1 mW는 계산된 결과이며, 계산은 로직 연산(演算) 이다.

; Semicolon ;

1. 리스트 중의 긴 항목(項目) 또는 콤마가 있는 항목의 분할(分割)

The system consists of three main components: extraction of the circuit netlist and parameters and RC line models from the layout; calculation of expected or average current waveforms drawn by the circuit at the contacts of the busses; and computation of average current densities in sections of the power and ground busses to estimate the amount of electromigration.

This paper covers the following topics: our SS-1 stepper; its overlay accuracy, including mask error; alignment offset control; a newly developed mask stage that improves this control; and some experimental results.

2. 콤마가 있는 주절(主節)의 분할

When SE is low, the date comes from normal D input; and when it is high, the data comes from scan-in-input.

some manufacturers call it a cassette or tray; but considering its function, we think "carrier" is a more appropriate term.

The deposition rate hardly depends at all on hydrogen gas pressure; but the deposition constant, k, is probably influenced by equipment-related factors, such as the method of heating and pumping speed.

3. 밀접(密接)히 관계된 두 절(節)의 분할

It has been observed that, above a value of 1, it becomes difficult or impossible to simultaneously print all feature types at the correct size; this can be used as a rule of thumb to determine the resolution limits of the different processes.

At a given supply voltage, the output of CMOS logic gates make rail-to-rail transitions; an approach to reducing the power consumption further is to reduce the voltage swing on large capacitance nodes.

NOTE 이 경우, 절(節)을 두 문장으로 나눌 수가 있다.

At a given supply voltage, the output of CMOS logic gates make rail-to-rail transitions. An approach to reducing the power consumption further is to reduce the voltage swing on large capacitance nodes.

PRACTICE

다음 문장 중 부적절한 콤마는 세미콜론으로 바꾸어라.

1. The open circles are for the pile-up model, and as you can see, the agreement is excellent.

2. This figure illustrates a number of key characteristics of the kink: The kink in I_D occurs approximately at a constant V_{DG} of 1.2 V, the size of the kink appears to increase with increasing V_{GS}, and the onset of the kink coincides with the appearance of I_{SG} and with a prominent rise in E_G, presumably due to hole collection by the gate.

3. Below the line, diffusion is dominant, and above, drift is dominant.

4. Unlike digital LSIs, most of the area of MMICs is occupied by passive elements, such as transmission lines, inductors, and capacitors, and reducing their size is the best way to miniaturize MMICs.

5. Circuit extraction is an important step in VLSI circuit design verification, it provides the link between the physical design and its verification phases.

6. AS you can see, when the phase is 160 °, the best-focus position does not shift at all, and the depth of focus is as wide as that without spherical aberration.

7. The data timing is ideally centered at zero and tracks the data bit rate, it is ideally ±0.75 ns at a data bit rate of 1.5 ns, and ±1.5 ns at a data bit rate of 3.0 ns.

Prepositions 6

빈칸을 적절한 전치사로 메꾸어라. 만일 필요 없다면 X로 메꾸어라.

REVIEW

a. X is comparable _________ Y.

b. X is similar _________ Y.

c. Sato *et al*. mention _________ two problems ...

d. X gives rise _________ Y.

e. X is characteristic _________ Y.

f. X is associated _________ Y.

g. X is suitable _________ Y.

h. X is suited _________ Y.

I. X is added _________ Y.

j. X affects _________ Y.

CHECK YOUR KNOWLEDGE

1. X arises _________ Y.
2. the variation _________ the width
3. X is made up _________ Y and Z.
4. X is injected _________ Y.
5. X is incorporated _________ Y.
6. This paper deals _________ X.
7. X compensates _________ Y.
8. X is consistent _________ Y. (Do not confuse this with "consist of.")
9. X takes Y _________ consideration.
10. The limit _________ X...

Section 7

problem with/of

measured vs. measurement

Bad Passives

know vs. find out

another vs. the other

to + -ing/Noun

maintain vs. remain

difference

saturate

because vs. since

Punctuation: Parentheses

Prepositions 7

problem with/of

POINT

어떤 일에 이상한 데, 불충분한 면, 또는 결점이 있는 (즉, 어떤 일에 문제가 있는) 경우, 흔히 [problem with]를 써서 설명한다.

problem with

Z에는 문제가 있다.	There is a **problem with** Z.
Z의 문제는 _____ 이다.	The **problem with Z** is (that) _____ .

BASIC PATTERNS

The problem with the car **is** the brakes.

The problem with the car **is that** the brakes do not function properly.

The problem with the car **can be solved by** replacing the brake pads.

GOOD EXAMPLES

× *The problem of this device is the cost of assembly.*

○ **The problem with this device** is the cost of assembly.

× *The problems of this method are the large line width and poor stability.*

○ **The problems with this method** are the large line width and poor stability.

× *The most serious problem in solid-oxide fuel cells employing a hydrocarbon as fuel is carbon deposition on the anode.*

○ **The most serious problem with** solid-oxide fuel cells employing a hydrocarbon as fuel is carbon deposition on the anode.

problem of Z = [Z 라는 문제]

The problem of the brakes can be solved by replacing the brake pads.

○ This leaves **the problem of how to** control the phase error in the delay lines.

○ These lasers feature fast switching and a wide tuning range, but they suffer from **the problem of mode hopping**.

measured vs. measurement

The **measured wavelength** was 400 nm. 파장(波長)을 재어보니 400 nm 이었다.	The **measurement wavelength** was 400 nm. 측정(測定)에는 400 nm의 파장을 썼다.

We measured the characteristics and obtained some results.

The characteristics were measured.	the results of the measurement

measured characteristics	measurement results

비슷한 표현 : calculated characteristics simulated characteristics	비슷한 표현 : calculation results simulation results

- ○ Figure 6 shows **simulated waveforms** of a 32-bit adder.
- ○ Table 3 compares the **simulated and measured power consumption** at a voltage of 0.8 V.
- ○ Based on the **calculated carrier distribution** under the threshold condition, we calculated the threshold current density.
- ○ The circles are **measured values.**
- ○ Figure 5 compares **measured and calculated** spectra for Structure A.
- ○ The calculations employed the **measured gain characteristics**.
- ○ Figure 2 shows some **measurement results** on fast tuning.
- ○ The **measurement results** show that the coupling efficiency is quite uniform across all the channels; and the **calculation results** indicate that it should be possible to make a CWDM module with over 10 channels.
- ○ The accuracy of the simulations was verified by comparing **simulation and measurement results.**

Bad Passives

POINT

[Occur], [remain], [appear]와 [disappear]는 자동사이며, **수동태는 없다.**
[Originate]는 타동사이기도 자동사이기도 하지만, 자동사 편이 자주 쓰인다.

occur

× *Anode degradation by carbon deposition is occurred.*

○ Carbon deposition causes the anode **to degrade**.

× *The electrolyte decomposition was occurred continuously.*

- 경우에 따라서는, 명사를 동사로 바꿈으로써 [be occurred]라는 부분이 생략 될 수 있다.

○ The electrolyte continuously **decomposed**.

originate in/from

NOTE [Originate]를 타동사로 쓰는 경우, 주어는 사람인 것에 주의하라. 예를 들면

Einstein **originated** the theory of relativity.

× *The incubation period is originated from the reduction in the amount of adsorbed oxygen.*

○ The incubation period **originates from** the reduction in the amount of adsorbed oxygen.

× *We compensated for the skew originated in the output cables.*

○ We compensated for the skew **originating in** the output cables.

remain

× *This method expands only narrow valleys. So, narrow ridges are remained.*

○ This method expands only narrow valleys. So, narrow ridges **remain**.

appear/disappear

× *The degradation is only appeared during impact stress.*

○ The degradation **only appears** during impact stress.

PRACTICE

틀린 수동태의 동사를 고쳐라

1. The variation in lasing frequency among the devices **is originated in** the fabrication process.

   ____

2. A 30-nm-thick layer of SiO_2 **was remained** on top.

   ____

3. The GaAs layer **may be disappeared** during overetching if the microwave power is too high.

   ____

4. Limit-cycle oscillations **is occurred**.

   ____

5. It is impossible to avoid the bandwidth limitation **originated from** the carrier response of the semiconductor.

   ____

6. A high power density enables **to be occurred** nonlinear optical effects.

   ____

7. The data stored in the selected memory cell **are appeared** on the bit lines.

   ____

8. This high value suggests that hydrogen passivation **is still remained.**

   ____

know vs. find out

What is 7 × 8?

상태: I know!
(그것을 알고 있다!)

행동: To find out ...
(그것을 알아내기 위해서는)

When you **know** something, you have the information (정보를 갖고 있다.)

When [알고 있다] means to get information (정보를 얻다), it is translated as "**find out**."

TYPICAL MISTAKES

× *To know whether or not the structure contains SiO_2, we analyzed the interior.*

○ **To find out** whether or not the structure contains SiO_2, ...

× *To obtain good control of the device characteristics, we must know how the oxidation proceeds.*

○ .. we must **find out** how the oxidation proceeds.

○ ...we must **gain a thorough understanding** of how the oxidation proceeds.

× *We can know which LSI chips are good by measuring their standby current at a low temperature.*

○ We **can find out/determine** which LSI chips are good by ...

GOOD EXAMPLES

○ **If we know** the surface potential (V_s), we can derive the thickness.

○ We **need to know** more about how these resists work.

○ We **know** that the defects contain oxygen.

○ **As you know**, it is important to reduce the power consumption of LSIs.

PRACTICE

빈칸을 [know]나 [find out]로 메꾸어라

1. We measured the change in weight of a calcium electrode to _______________ whether or not electrochemical dissolution occurs.
2. To fully understand self-heating-related phenomena, we need to _______________ the temperature of the device.
3. It is very important to _______________________ how these services are actually used if we hope to reduce their environmental load.
4. We need to _________________ what concentration of surfactant is needed to make water miscible in hexane.
5. We also ran tests in Hokkaido to _________________ how the battery pack would perform in intense cold.
6. Plasma containing a large amount of fluoride gas does not etch Ta. To ___________________ why, we added a small amount of fluoride gas to CI plasma and investigated its influence.
7. If we ________________ the width and length, we can estimate the height using this relationship.
8. To ___________________ what is happening during the incubation period before deposition begins, we analyzed the surface of deposited film.
9. We _______________ that AH_3 reacts with Group-III sources.
10. Activation energy is a useful parameter for characterizing reactions. So, we need to ___________________ what the value is to clarify the degradation process.

another vs. the other

another

DEFINITION: 한가지 것에 언급한 후, 같은 종류의 **다른 것**, 또는 다른 종류의 것에 언급하는 경우, [another]를 쓴다.

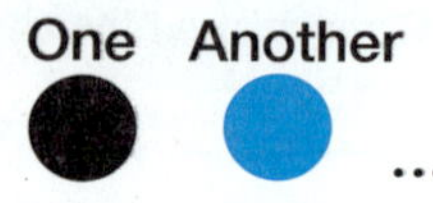

- One big advantage is that we do not need a phase control region. **Another** is easy stabilization of the wavelength.
- For identification, the sensor LSI captures a fingerprint image. If the quality is not good enough, the parameters are changed and **another** image is captured.
- Figure 6 shows the results of accelerated aging tests to estimate the lifetime. In **another** test, the cells were charged intermittently ...

[The another]는 영어가 아닌 것에 주의하자.

the other(s)

DEFINITION: **특정한 그룹**에 관해 이야기 하는 경우, 그 그룹의 일부에 관해 말한 후 나머지 부분을 말할 때 [the other(s)]를 쓴다.

Mentioned item(s)

The other(s)

특정한 그룹

- Two laser beams are fed into this loop. One is a reference, and **the other** is a pump laser.
- There are two ways to expand the exposure area. One is to move the mirror back and forth, and **the other** is to move the mask and wafer.
- There are various ways of depositing copper, such as sputtering, plating, and CVD. CVD has several big advantages over **the others**.
- When one of the four transistor is active, **the others** are inactive.

to + -ing/Noun

[Approach], [contribute]와 [key] 뒤의 [to]는 전치사이다. 전치사의 목적어는 명사이거나 동명사이며, 동사가 아니다.

approach to improving/improvement

× *We have developed a new approach to improve resist patterns.*

○ We have developed a new **approach to improving** resist patterns.

× *Our approach to shorten the switching time is explained below.*

○ Our **approach to shortening** the switching time is explained below.

× *We have devised another approach to prevent oscillations.*

○ We have devised another **approach to preventing** oscillations.

contribute to improving/improvement

× *This contributes to improve the reliability.*

○ This **contributes to improving** the reliability.

× *Our goal is to contribute to create an environmentally friendly society.*

○ Our goal is to **contribute to the creation** of an environmentally friendly society.

× *This contributes to reduce CO_2 emissions.*

○ This **contributes to a reduction** in CO_2 emissions.

key to improving/improvement

× *Sealing with polyimide is the key to improve the yield.*

○ Sealing with polyimide is the **key to improving** the yield.

× *These technologies are the key to make ultralow-power LSIs.*

○ These technologies are the **keys to making** ultralow-power LSIs.

× *This is the key to reduce roughness.*

○ This is the **key to reducing** roughness.

maintain vs. remain

remain

[**Remain**]은 변화하지 않는는 상태가 이어진다는 간단한 아이디어를 나타내고 있다.

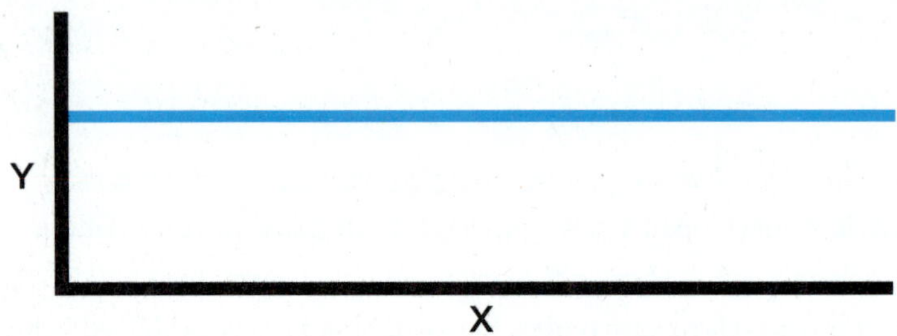

- The chamber is not heated and **remains** at room temperature.
- This mechanism ensures that the output power **remains** constant.

maintain

[**Maintain**]은 본래 액티브이며, 같은 상태로 유지하기 위한 행동을 가리킨다. 이 단어가 적절히 쓰이고 있다면, [무엇이 무엇을 유지하는가] 또 [무엇이 무엇에서 유지되는가]란 질문에 답하는 것이다.

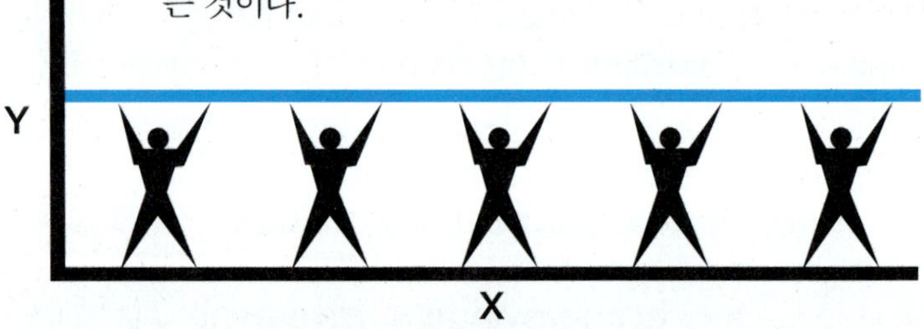

- A capacitor in the loop filter **maintains** the control voltage of the oscillator.
- The temperature is raised to 35℃, while the pressure **is maintained** at 7.5 MPa with a pressure-control valve.

[변화 없음] 이란 것 만을 적고 싶은 경우,
[maintain]은 적절치 않다.

TYPICAL MISTAKES

remain

PATTERN 1 remain + 형용사

× *Good electroabsorption characteristics are maintained.*

○ The electroabsorption characteristics **remain good**.

PATTERN 2 remain the same

× *The center of the delay time distribution shifts to a larger value, but the critical delay (largest value) is maintained.*

○ ... but the critical delay (largest value) **remains the same**.

PATTERN 3 remain + 수치(數值)

× *A current gain of over 20 is maintained.*

○ The current gain **remains over 20**.

PRACTICE

[Maintain]을 [remain]으로 바꾸어라.

1. A constant output power is maintained.

   ____

2. When 1530 nm ≤ λ ≤ 1570 nm, the extinction ratio is maintained over 13 dB.

   ____

3. The Ni and Ti contents were maintained during the ion-exchange process.

   ____

4. The optical quality of the output light should be maintained, even after thousands of circulations.

   ____

5. The steep energy profile around the edge is maintained.

   ____

6. The return loss maintained a sufficiently high value.

   ____

difference

difference between X and Y

There is a a difference **between** the valley and the coast.

There is a difference **between** the temperature of the valley and that of the coast.

10℃

Valley 15℃

Coast 25℃

There is a difference **between** the temperatures of the valley and the coast.

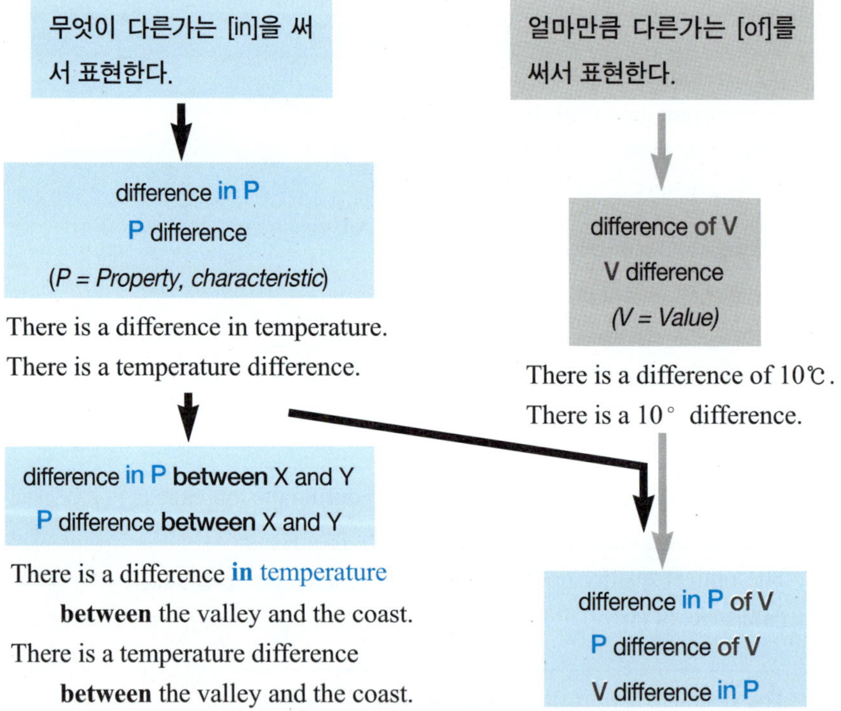

무엇이 다른가는 [in]을 써서 표현한다.

difference in P
P difference
(*P = Property, characteristic*)

There is a difference in temperature.
There is a temperature difference.

difference in P **between** X and Y
P difference **between** X and Y

There is a difference **in** temperature **between** the valley and the coast.
There is a temperature difference **between** the valley and the coast.

얼마만큼 다른가는 [of]를 써서 표현한다.

difference of V
V difference
(*V = Value*)

There is a difference of 10℃.
There is a 10° difference.

difference in P of V
P difference of V
V difference in P

There is a difference **in** temperature of 10℃.
There is a temperature difference of 10℃.
There is a 10° difference **in** temperature.

difference **in P** of V **between** X and Y
P difference of V **between** X and Y
V difference **in P** **between** X and Y

There is a difference **in** temperature **of** 10℃ **between** the valley and the coast.
There is a temperature difference **of** 10℃ **between** the valley and the coast.
There is a 10° difference **in** temperature **between** the valley and the coast.

PRACTICE

빈 칸을 [in] 이나 [between]으로 메꾸어라.

1. The difference ________ the low and medium voltages is only 0.1 V.
2. There is a 10-dB difference ________ noise level ________ these two places near the road.
3. We speculate that this difference ________ characteristics ________ Ru- and Fe-doped samples could be due to a difference ________ current-blocking properties.
4. We obtained a difference ________ maximum matching rate ________ only 0.05.
5. The refractive-index difference ________ the core and the cladding is 0.4%.
6. The difference ________ the free energies of reactions (1) and (3) is very small.
7. There is a small difference ________ free energy ________ reactions (1) and (3).
8. The calculations did not take into account the difference ________ reflection angle ________ rays due to the curvature of the mirror.
9. This circuit detects the difference ________ the two outputs of the amplifier.
10. The difference ________ reflectivity can be explained by the roughness of the multilayer.
11. There is a difference ________ output power ________ less than 1.0 dB channels.

saturate

다음 예를 음미해보면, [saturate]의 기본적 이미지가 파악된다.

Ex. 1: 스펀지에 많은 물을 주고, 그 이상 흡수할 수 없는 상태가 된 경우, 스펀지는 물로 포화(飽和) 되어있다고 한다.
The sponge **is saturated** with water.

Not saturated

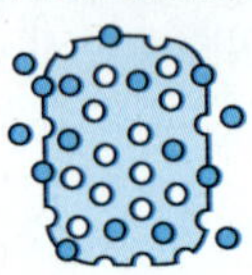

saturated

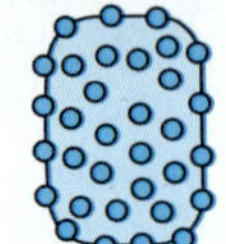

Ex. 2: The market **is saturated** 란 소비능력(消費能力)의 한계까지 제품이 시장에 공급되고, 매상고(賣上高)가 올라 괴로운 것이다.

Ex. 3: 물이 용해(溶解)할 수 있는 한계까지 식염(食鹽)을 물에 넣으면, 포화(飽和) 식염수가 된다. **a saturated** salt solution

Ex. 1에는, 물이 공급되어 스펀지가 한계까지 물을 받아들인다.
Ex. 2에는, 제품이 공급되어, 시장이 한계까지 제품을 받아들인다.
Ex. 3에는, 소금이 공급되어, 물이 한계까지 소금을 받아들인다.

위의 경우에서 보았듯이, [saturate]라는 개념에 두 요소(要素)가 있다:
(1) 무엇인가가 **공급되고 있다**.
(2) 받아들이는 측(側)의 받아들이는 양이 **증가**하여 **한계**에 도달한다.
[Saturate]의 의미는 이것에 바탕을 두고 있다.

예를 들면, 증폭기(增幅器)에 전압을 입력하면, 그것이 증폭되어 출력되지만, 어느 치(値) 이상의 전압이 입력되면, 출력 전압이 포화되어 일정치(一定値)가 된다.
The output voltage **saturates** at V_x.

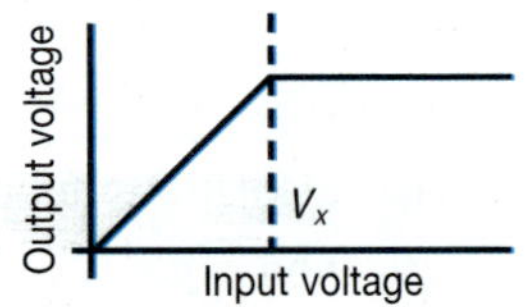

The output voltage is **saturated** at input voltages above V_x.

POINT

[Saturate]는 [**공급(供給)**]과 [**수용(受容)**]의 관계가 있는 것 이외에는 쓸 수가 없다. 예를 들면 TV채널의 시청률이 최고점에 오른 것에 [saturated]는 쓰이지 않는다.

TYPICAL MISTAKES

× *As the input energy increases, <u>the ON/OFF ratio</u> increases rapidly and then <u>saturates</u>.*

- 비율은 [수용량(受容量)]이 아니다.

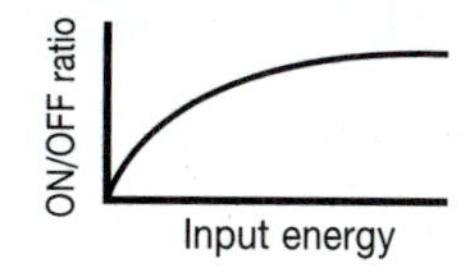

○ As the input energy increases, the ON/OFF ratio increases rapidly and then **levels off**.

× *The current gain drops initially, and then <u>the degradation appears to saturate</u> at around 300 hours.*

- 저하(低下)의 정도 및 전류 게인을 모두 감소하고 있기 때문에 [saturate]와 정반대(正反對) 이다. 또, 저하(低下)는 [수용량]이 아니다.

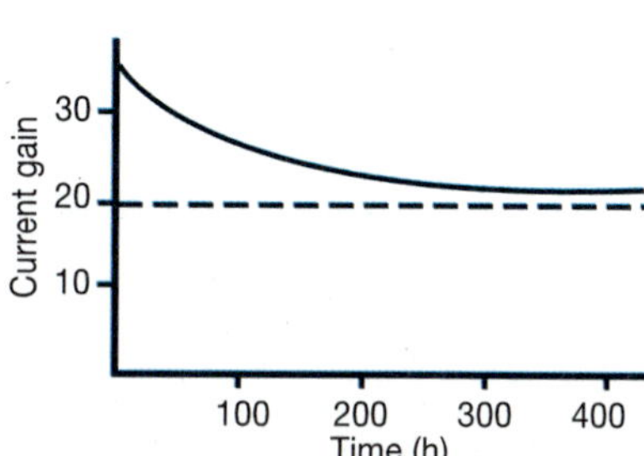

○ The current gain drops initially, and then **levels off** at around 300 hours.

× *The delay starts increasing at -1.5 V, and <u>saturates</u> at a voltage of around -0.4 V.*

- 지연은 [수용량]이 아니다.

○ The delay starts increasing at -1.5 V and **reaches a maximum** at a voltage of around -0.4 V.

× *The <u>height</u> of the peak increases with and finally <u>saturates</u> when $V_f = 1.5$ V.*

- 높이는 [수용량]이 아니다.

○ The height of the peak increases with V_f and finally **reaches a maximum** when $V_f = 1.5$ V.

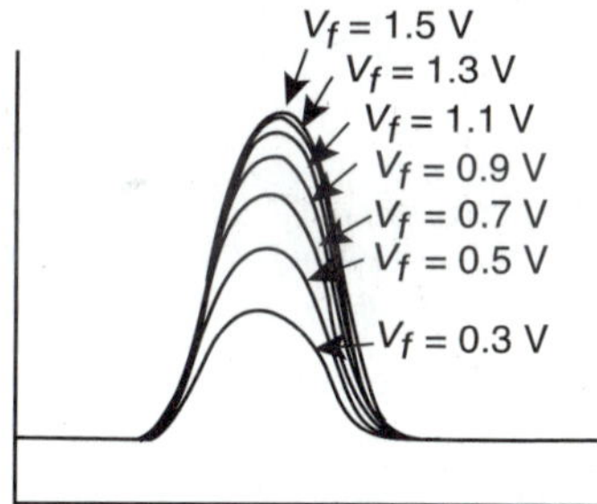

GOOD EXAMPLES

○ The drain <u>current</u> increases with bias and **saturates** when the bias reaches 3 V.

○ The SH <u>power</u> **saturates** when the input power is increased.

○ The PC <u>market</u> **will be saturated** in 2 years, and the use of personal digital assistants will increase rapidly due to their low cost and portability.

because vs. since

because

[Because] 로 시작하는 절(節)은, 원인을 강조하기 위해 흔히 주절(主節) 뒤에 둔다.

NOTE 1 이것은 엄밀한 규칙이 아니고 영미인(英美人) 작성한 문장에도 [because]로 시작하는 것이 보인다.

NOTE 2 [Because of]라는 표현은 위의 논의(論議) 밖이다.

○ For mobile equipment, power efficiency is the top priority **because** it determines battery life.

○ This laser is easy to tune **because** it needs only one tuning current.

TYPICAL MISTAKES

× *Because the coefficient varies almost linearly with wavelength, it is easy to estimate.*

○ The coefficient is easy to estimate **because** it varies almost linearly with wavelength.

× *It is very important to reduce the leakage current since it accounts for most of the power dissipation.*

○ It is very important to reduce the leakage current **because** it accounts for most of the power dissipation.

× *We selected Okinawa and Hokkaido as test sites since they represent environmental extremes.*

○ We selected Okinawa and Hokkaido as test sites **because** they represent environmental extremes.

[Because]로 시작하는 절(節) 자체는 완전한 문장이 아니다.

× *The solution is to make the coefficients of thermal expansion of the chip and the film almost the same. Because a large difference between them reduces the adhesion.*

○ The solution is to make the coefficients of thermal expansion of the chip and the film almost the same **because** a large difference between them reduces the adhesion.

× *Monolithic integration will be a key technology. <u>Because</u> it enables active and passive devices to be combined on a small chip with few optical alignment points.*

○ Monolithic integration will be a key technology because it enables active and passive devices to be combined on a small chip with few optical alignment points.

그러나, 질문의 답으로서, [because]를 시작하는 절(節)을 단독으로 써도 된다.

○ Why do we integrate IC chips on a PLC substrate? **Because** it results in smaller, cheaper devices.

since

[Since]로 시작하는 원인의 절(節)은, 결과로서의 주절(主節)을 강조하기 위해, 흔히 주절(主節) 앞에 둔다.

NOTE 1 이것은 엄밀한 규칙이 아니고, 오히려 영미인(英美人)이 작성한 문장에 보이는 경향이다.

○ **Since** the clamping force is greater than the buckling force, no adhesive is necessary.

○ **Since** the Arrhenius plot is roughly linear, we can conclude that the drop in capacity is due to a chemical reaction.

TYPICAL MISTAKES

× *<u>Because</u> no anti-reflection coating was deposited on the back of the substrate, there are multiple reflections from the substrate.*

○ **Since** no anti-reflection coating was deposited on the back of the substrate, there are multiple reflections from the substrate.

× *<u>Because</u> electrons have a high mobility, they are quickly swept out of the collection layer.*

○ **Since** electrons have a high mobility, they are quickly swept out of the collection layer.

× *The encoder is made with low-threshold logic gates <u>since</u> it is on a critical path.*

○ **Since** the encoder is on a critical path, it is made with low-threshold logic gates.

( ) Parentheses ( )

NOTE 왼쪽 괄호 앞에 스페이스를 넣어라. 피어리드, 콤마 등이 뒤에 있는 경우를 제외하고, 오른쪽 괄호 뒤에도 스페이스를 넣어라.

1. 리스트, 라벨, 수치(數値)

Six chips (a protocol chip, six 64-kbit SRAMs for text/graphics frame buffering, and four custom chips for video decompression) provide the interface between...

There are three inputs (A, B, C) and two outputs (D, E). The sum of the n- and p-MOSFET threshold voltages (V_{tn}=0.7 V, V_{tp}= -0.9 V) is greater than the supply voltage.

NOTE 리스트는 괄호를 에워싼 경우, [and]를 쓸 필요가 없다.

2. 두자어(頭字語)

...silicon-on-insulator (SOI) technology ...

Coding methods have been devised that efficiently combine linear predictive coding (LPC) and sinusoidal coding.

3. 기호(記號)

... the threshold voltage (V_{th}) of the device...

For each offset (k) with respect to the original sampling grid,...

이 경우 괄호 대신 콤마를 써도 좋다 (94페이지를 참조할 것).

4. 코멘트와 주석(注釋)

A very large λ will satisfy all the timing constraints (if they can be satisfied) but will result in poor values of W.

Compressed YIQ video uses a ping-pong scheme (one pair of memories for Y and one pair for IQ), providing...

Each new generation (about every 3 years) of microprocessor has tended to be about three times faster than its predecessor.

5. 참고문헌, 참조개소관련(参照箇所關聯)

In the 21064 processor (Fig. #), the clock strip runs down the center ...

.. it corresponds to the method in which the hand model was calibrated (see[11]), which enables both the calibration and tracking procedures to...

Prepositions 7

빈칸을 적절한 전치사로 메꾸어라. 만일 필요없다면, X로 메꾸어라.

REVIEW

a. X is incorporated __________ Y.

b. X arises __________ Y.

c. This paper is concerned __________ X.

d. As a result __________ X, ...

e. X is made up __________ Y and Z.

f. This paper deals __________ X.

g. This paper discusses __________ a new approach...

h. X is different __________ Y.

I. X influences __________ Y.

j. X has an influence __________ Y.

CHECK YOUR KNOWLEDGE

1. X is inferior __________ Y.
2. X leads __________ Y.
3. X brings __________ Y. [=cause]
4. This paper focuses __________ X.
5. The upper/lower bound __________ Y...
6. __________ consequence,....
7. X is effective __________ doing something.
8. X is __________ accordance __________ Y.
9. oscillations __________ the conductance
10. I will talk __________ (a subject).

Section 8

each

not A or B

fluctuation vs. variation

with -ing

proportion(al)

monotonous vs. monotonic

whose

flow

against

Punctuation: Capitals

Punctuation: Dash

Punctuation: Slash

Prepositions 8

each

POINT

[Each]는 **단수(單數) 명사**와 함께 사용한다. 또 [each] 앞에 [the]는 붙이지 않는다.

each + 단수명사

TYPICAL MISTAKES

× *Large programs and data sets are stored on a server, and <u>each PCs download</u> them when necessary.*

○ Large programs and data sets are stored on a server, and **each PC downloads** them when necessary.

× *The peaks of <u>each output spectra</u> are flat.*

○ The peak of **each output spectrum** is flat.

× *<u>Each devices have</u> sufficient wavelength accuracy.*

○ **Each device has** sufficient wavelength accuracy.

~~the~~ each

TYPICAL MISTAKES

× *<u>The each</u> spot-size converter region is 300 μm long and 0.6 μm wide.*

○ **Each** spot-size converter region is 300 μm long and 0.6 μm wide.

× *The phase of <u>the each</u> longitudinal mode is locked with that of the RF input signal.*

○ The phase of **each** longitudinal mode is locked with that of the RF input signal.

not A or B

A와 B라는 두 물체를 생각해 보자. 양쪽이 있으면 [A and B] 라고 한다. 어느것도 아닌 경우, [not A or B]라고 한다. 한편 [not A and B]는 아래에 보여 지듯이 세 케이스가 포함된다.

A and B

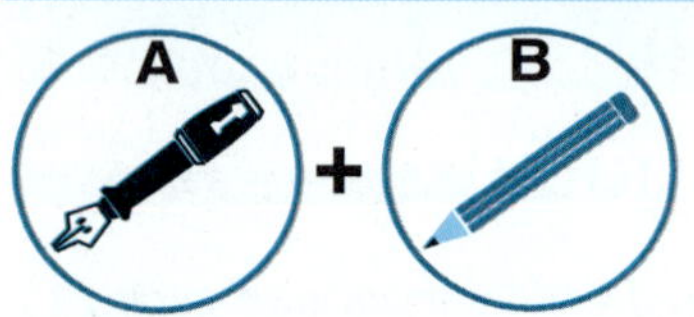

I have a pen **and** a pencil.

not (A and B)

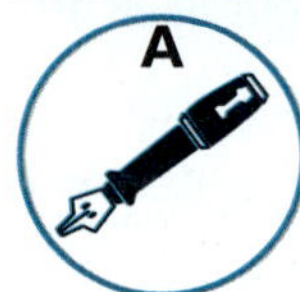

I do **not** have a pen **and** a pencil.
I have only a pen.

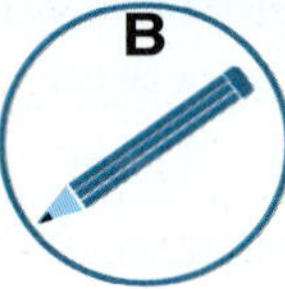

I do **not** have a pen **and** a pencil.
I have only a pencil.

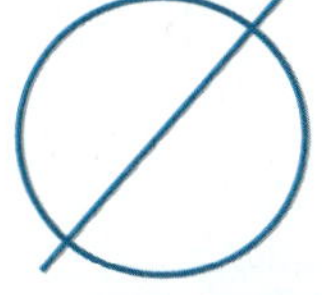

I do **not** have a pen **or** a pencil.
(= I do not have a pen, and I do not have a pencil.)

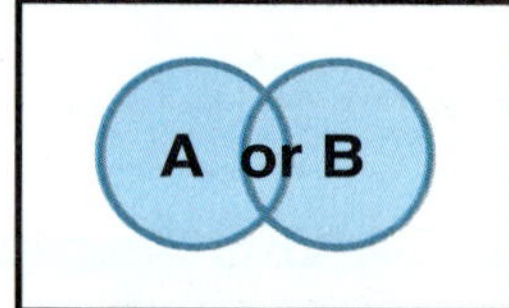

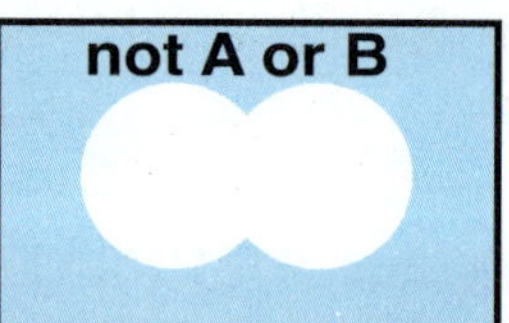

TYPICAL MISTAKES

× *This design does* <u>*not*</u> *depend on the size of the device* <u>*and*</u> *the type of glass.*

○ This design does **not** depend on the size of the device or the type of glass.

× *One patient with brain damage could* <u>*not*</u> *draw objects from short-term memory* <u>*and*</u> *recall the color of objects from long-term memory.*

○ One patient with brain damage could **not** draw objects from short-term memory or recall the color of objects from long-term memory.

NOTE [Without]도 부정적(否定的)인 단어이므로, 어느것도 없는 경우에 [without A or B]를 쓴다.

× We obtained a completely flat surface without any islands and holes.
○ We obtained a completely flat surface **without** any islands or holes.

× Resist patterns rinsed with alcohol can be dried without collapse and deformation.
○ Resist patterns rinsed with alcohol can be dried **without** collapse or deformation.

문장의 주어인 경우

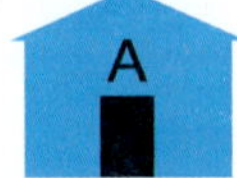

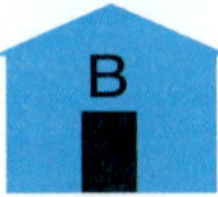

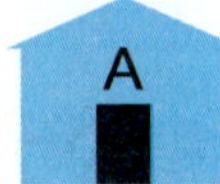

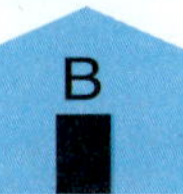

○ Both houses **are** red.

○ A and B **are** red.

× *Both houses are not red.*
○ **Neither** house **is** red.

× *A and B are not red.*
○ **Neither** A **nor** B **is** red.

both ... are not  neither ... is

TYPICAL MISTAKES

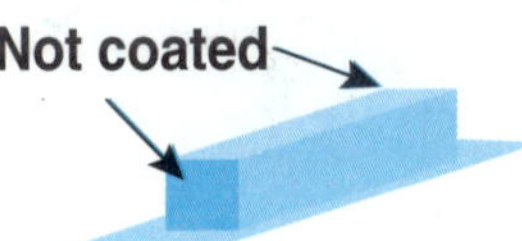

× *The front and rear facets of the laser were not coated. (Both facets of the laser were not coated.)*
○ **Neither** the front **nor** the rear facet of the laser was coated. (**Neither** facet of the laser **was** coated.)

× *Both Solvent A and Solvent B cannot dissolve the base polymer.*
○ **Neither** Solvent A **nor** Solvent B can dissolve the base polymer.

× *When both pump pulses are not input into the comparator, the polarization of the probe pulse is preserved.*
○ When **neither** pump pulse **is** input into the comparator, the polarization of the probe pulse is preserved.

fluctuation vs. variation

fluctuation

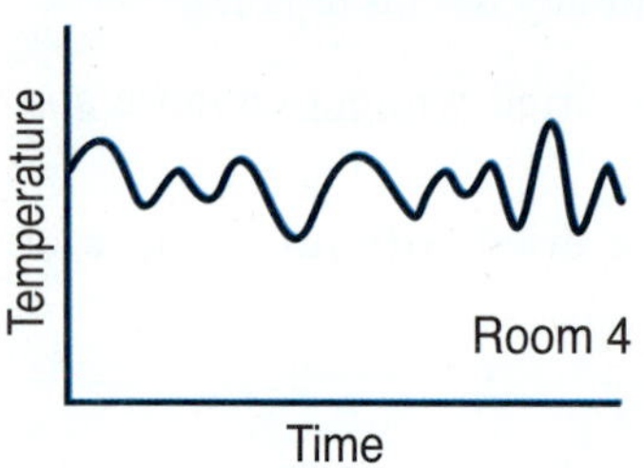

DEFINITION: [Fluctuations]는, **하나의 사물에** 관해 쓰며, 그 특성의 연속적이면서 불규칙한 변화를 가리킨다. 규칙적이라면, [oscillations]를 쓴다. [Fluctuations]는, 어떤 특성이 **시간과 더불어** 변화하고 있음을 의미한다.

- The **temperature** of Room 4 **fluctuates.**
- The **fluctuations in the temperature** of <u>Room 4</u> are very small.
- The **temperature fluctuations** for <u>Room 4</u> are very small.

NOTE [Fluctuations]는 통상 복수형(複數形)을 쓴다.

variation

DEFINITION: [Variation]는 다른 것을 가리킨다.

1. 몇 가지 사상(事象)에 관하여 어떤 특성의 차이 (Fig. A).
2. 한 쪽의 변수(變數)의 변화에 따르고, 다른 쪽의 변수가 변화한다 (Fig. B).

어느 케이스에 있어서도, [variation]은 자주 **최대치(最大値)**와 **최소치(最小値)**의 차이를 가리킨다.

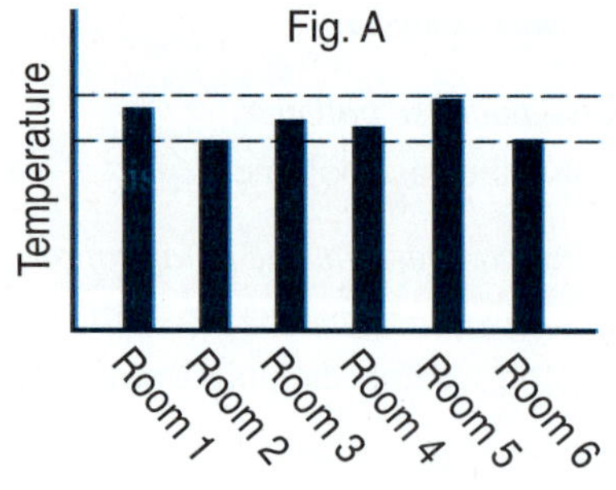

- The **temperature varies** among the rooms.
- There is a small **variation in temperature** among the rooms.
- The **temperature variation** among the rooms is 7℃.

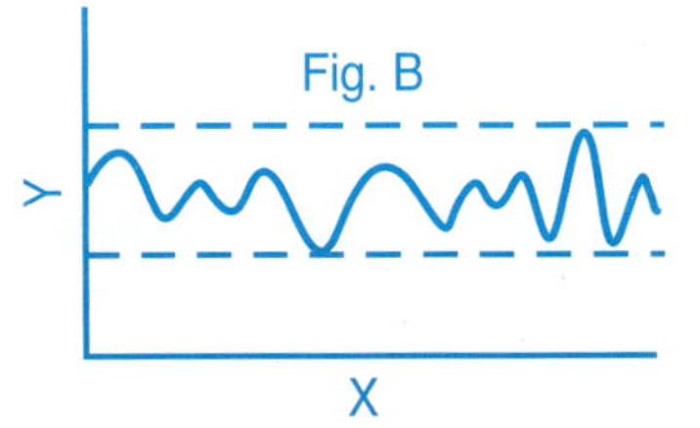

- ○ The **variations in temperature** for Room 3 are large.
- ○ The **temperature variation** for Room 3 is large.

GOOD EXAMPLES

■ FLUCTUATIONS

- ○ Datacom equipment should have a capacitor connected to the power line to suppress **voltage fluctuations**.
- ○ To reduce the change in wavelength due to **temperature fluctuations**, we employ a mechanical offset to compensate for the fluctuations.
- ○ ...**fluctuations in** the local magnetic field ...
- ○ The noise arises from **fluctuations in** the ground potential.

■ VARIATION

- ○ The **variation in received power** among the channels is less than 1 dB.
- ○ This technique planarizes large patterns, with the **variation in thickness** being as small as ±0.43%.
- ○ The image is affected by noise and **local variations in intensity and contrast**.

TYPICAL MISTAKES

- × *The limiting amplifier reduces packet-to-packet power fluctuations.*
  - 이 문장은 패키트 사이의 파워의 차이에 관한 것으로, [fluctuations]는 적절치 않다. (패키트: 통신 데이터의 전송단위)
- ○ The limiting amplifier reduces **packet-to-packet power variations.**
- × *The roughness results in line-width fluctuations.*
  - 선(線)의 폭(幅)은 시간과 함께 변화하지 않는다.
- ○ The roughness results in **variations in line width.**

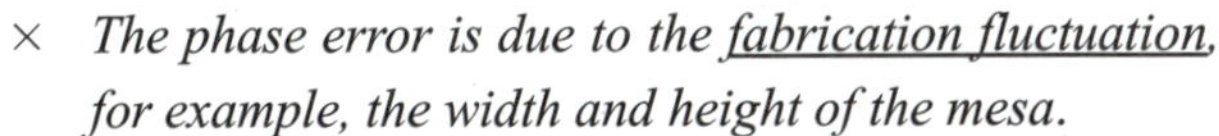

- × *The phase error is due to the fabrication fluctuation, for example, the width and height of the mesa.*
- ○ The phase error is due to **process variations**, for example, variations in the width and height of the mesas.

with -ing

PROBLEM 1 다음 문장은 영어가 되어 있지 않다.

× *The output power decreases* ***with increasing the*** *frequency.*

× *The output power decreases* ***with increasing of*** *frequency.*

먼저, 올바른 영어를 보자.

○ The output power increases **with wavelength**.

위의 문장에서, [with]는 전치사이며, [wavelength]는 전치사의 목적어 이다.

다음 문장을 생각해 보자.

○ The output power decreases **with** increasing **frequency**.

마찬가지로, 이 문장에서 [with]는 전치사이며, [frequency]는 전치사의 목적어 이다. 그런데, [increasing]의 품사는 무엇일까? [increasing]은 [frequency]를 묘사하는 형용사 이다.

이 설명에서 알 수 있듯이, 위의 틀린 문장의 문제: (1) 형용사와 명사 사이에는 [the]를 넣어서는 안 된다.. (2) 형용사 뒤에 [of]를 넣어서는 안 된다.

TYPICAL MISTAKES

× *The thickness of the film decreases linearly with increasing the pressure.*

○ The thickness of the film decreases linearly **with increasing pressure**.

× *The degradation of the battery cell accelerated with increasing of charging voltage.*

○ The degradation of the battery cell accelerated **with increasing charging voltage**.

NOTE [With]의 이 사용법을 쓰는 경우, [with] 뒤의 부분은 언제나 매우 심플하다. 더욱 복잡한 표현을 하고 싶은 경우는, 대신에 [as]를 쓰는 편이 좋다.

× *The hydrogen absorption-desorption properties improve with increasing degree of dispersion of the TiFeMn phase.*

○ The hydrogen absorption-desorption properties improve **as** the degree of dispersion of the TiFeMn phase **increases**.

× *The bandgap of silicon decreases with increasing strain induced by oxidation.*

○ The bandgap of silicon decreases **as** the strain induced by oxidation **increases**.

PROBLEM 2	[With keeping], [with maintaining], [with changing], [with satisfying]등의 표현은 영어가 되어 있지 않다.

A. 이 문제는 때때로 [while]을 써서 해결할 수 있다.

~~with -ing~~

while

× *We changed the power of the data signals with keeping the power of the dummy signals constant.*

○ We changed the power of the data signals **while keeping** the power of the dummy signals constant.

× *The relationship between peak output voltage and bandwidth was measured with changing the input power of the laser.*

○ The relationship between peak output voltage and bandwidth was measured **while changing** the input power of the laser.

B. 이 문제는 [**without changing**] 또는 [**without affecting**]를 써서 해결 할 수가 있다.

~~with -ing~~

without changing ...
without affecting ...

× *This technique improves the operating speed with maintaining the static performance of the circuit.*

○ This technique improves the operating speed **without affecting** the static performance of the circuit.

× *To boost the speed, the base and collector layers are thinned with maintaining the base sheet resistance.*

○ To boost the speed, the base and collector layers are thinned **without changing** the base sheet resistance.

× *It is not easy to further enhance the bandwidth of the output buffers with maintaining the voltage gain.*

○ It is not easy to further enhance the bandwidth of the output buffers **without affecting** the voltage gain.

C. 그러나 흔히 이 문제점이 생기는 원인은, 문장의 구조가 매우 나쁜데 있으며, 해결법으로서는 **기본문법을 공부해서, 문장을 작성하여 고치는 것**이다.

proportion(al)

in proportion to
전치사 + 명사 + to

~~in proportional to~~ NOT ENGLISH!

GOOD EXAMPLES

- The current of a macrocell increases **in proportion** to its bandwidth.
- The power decreases **in proportion** to the square of the supply voltage.
- The processing time scales **in proportion** to the size of the image.

be proportional to
be + 형용사 + to

NOTE 이것은 다음 표현과 같은 구조를 갖고 있다.
be equal to
be identical to

GOOD EXAMPLES

- The processing time **is proportional to** the bit length.
- The CMOS power consumption **is proportional to** the clock frequency.
- The resistance of a via **is inversely proportional** to the square of the diameter.
- The power consumption involved in physically transporting everyone to one spot **is roughly proportional** to the distance.

monotonous vs. monotonic

POINT

거의 모든 한영사전에는 [**단조로운**]을 [monotonous]라고만 번역 되어 있지만, 기술영어에서 쓰는 것은 이 단어가 아니고 [monotonic]임에 주의하자.

monotonous

DEFINITION: 무엇인가가 **monotonous** 하다는 것은, 그것은 언제나 일정한 패턴을 되풀이 하는 것이며, 매우 **지루하다**는 이미지가 있다.

- Most factory jobs are very **monotonous**.
- The rain dripped **monotonously** from the trees.

monotonic

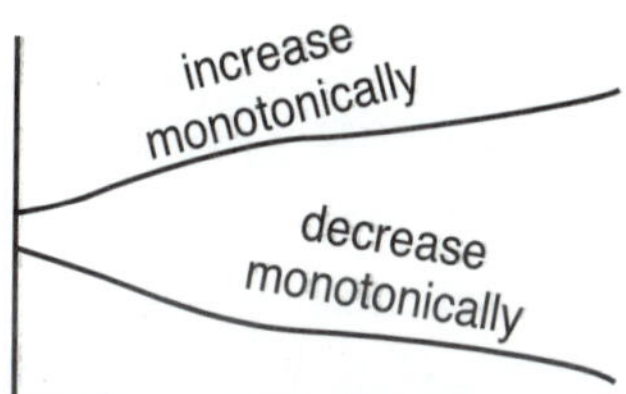

DEFINITION: 무엇인가가 **monotonically 증가(增加) 한다**는 것은, 어떤 치(値)도 그 앞의 치(値)보다 작지 않다는 것을 의미하며, 즉, 어떤 점(点)에서도 감소하지 않는 것이다. 마찬가지로, 무엇인가가 **monotonically 감소(減少) 한다**는 것은, 어떤 치(値)도 그 앞의 치(値)보다 크지 않다는 것을 의미한다. 즉, 어떤 점에서도 증가하지 않는 것이다.

- The standard deviation **increases monotonically**.
- The **monotonic increase** in resistivity with annealing time...
- As the V/III ratio increases, the C^{12} concentration **decreases monotonically**.
- The insertion loss **rises monotonically** to －5 dB as the frequency increases from 40 MHz to 100 GHz.

whose

POINT

기술영어에서는 [whose]는 별로 쓰지 않는다. 그 대신, [with] 나 [which]를 써 보자.

~~whose~~  **with ... of**

× ... *a voltage* <u>*whose*</u> *amplitude is more than 2 V*

○ ... a voltage **with** <u>an amplitude</u> of more than 2 V

PRACTICE

[Whose]를 [with... of...]로 바꾸어라.

1. The media converter emits a signal <u>whose wavelength is 1300 nm</u>.

   ____.

2. We can generate fast electrical pulses <u>whose width is less than 30 ps</u>.

   ____.

3. An acceleration voltage of 100 kV produces a fine beam <u>whose diameter is about 6 nm</u>.

   ____.

~~whose~~  **with ... that**

× ... *a new mask* <u>*whose*</u> *phase corresponds to the spherical aberration*

○ ... a new mask **with** <u>a phase</u> **that** corresponds to the spherical aberration

PRACTICE

[Whose]를 [with.. that...]로 바꾸어라.

4. Operation is very difficult for baseband data signals <u>whose frequencies extend down to several kilohertz</u>.

   ____.

5. We used a toothed planar antenna <u>whose teeth correspond to frequencies from 150 GHz to 2.4 THz</u>.

   ____.

6. We are designing a converter <u>whose capacitors are fabricated on the chip</u>.

   ____.

  **which**

× ... this material, whose melting point is 32℃, ...

○ .. this material, which has a melting point of 32℃,...

PRACTICE

[Whose]를 [which]로 바꾸어라.

7. Fixed wireless access, whose top speed is 622 Mbit/s, was introduced in 199.

    ____.

8. The chip is packaged in a butterfly-type module, whose size the same as that of a standard LD module.

    ____.

9. The image rejection ratio is 49 dB, whose value satisfies the specifications for short-range wireless systems.

    ____.

~~whose~~  **for which**

× *In this experiment, we used ELTRAN SOI-Epi wafers, whose resistivity can be precisely controlled.*

○ In this experiment, we used ELTRAN SOI-Epi wafers, **for which** the resistivity can be precisely controlled.

PRACTICE

[Whose]를 [for which]로 바꾸어라.

10. This prevents the switches from using baseband signals, whose DC level is not usually 0 V.

    ____.

11. Electrons with energies of 10-50 eV, whose mean free paths are from one-half to a few nanometers long, are dominant.

    ____.

12. This new method was used to characterize a transistor whose electrical properties had been measured beforehand.

    ____.

flow

POINT

수순(手順)이나 과정(프로세스)등은, 일본어로 [프로-]라고 말하기도 하지만, 그것을 [flow]라고 번역해서는 안 된다.

~~flow~~ → **procedure**

BASIC PATTERNS

Figure 3 **illustrates/shows the XXX procedure.**
Figure 3 **shows the steps in the XXX procedure.**
in the XXX procedure (Fig. 3), first ...

× *Figure 3 shows the flow of image adjustment.*
○ Figure 3 **illustrates** the image adjustment **procedure**.

× *Figure 6 is a diagram of the conventional testing flow.*
○ Figure 6 shows **the steps in** the conventional testing **procedure**.

× *Figure 8 shows a flow of matching steps performed in the processing array.*
○ Figure 8 **illustrates** the matching **procedure** performed by the processing array.

× *The flow of measurements is shown in Fig. 5. First, electrons are stored in the memory node ...*
○ In the measurement **procedure** (Fig. 5), first, electrons are stored in the memory node ...

flow chart

BASIC PATTERNS

Figure 3 shows a flow chart of the XXX.

× *Figure 7 shows a flow of the image enhancement algorithm.*
○ Figure 7 **shows a flow chart of the** image enhancement algorithm.

× *Figure 6 is a diagram of the conventional testing flow.*
○ Figure 6 **shows a flow chart of the** conventional testing procedure.

fabrication process

BASIC PATTERNS

Figure 6 illustrates/shows the fabrication process.

Figure 6 illustrates the procedure for fabricating XXX.

Figure 6 shows the (main) steps in the fabrication process.

Figure 6 shows the (main) steps in the fabrication of XXX.

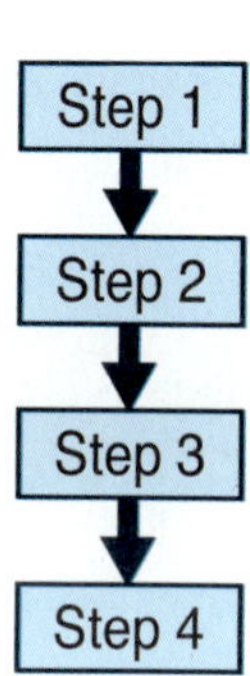

× *Figure 4 shows the flow of a fabrication process.*

○ Figure 4 **shows the fabrication process**.

○ Figure 4 **shows the steps in the fabrication process**.

× *Figure 5 shows the sensor fabrication process flow.*

○ Figure 5 **illustrates the procedure for fabricating** a sensor.

× *Figure 9 shows the outline of process flow to fabricate buried optical waveguides.*

○ Figure 9 **shows the main steps in the fabrication of** a buried optical waveguide.

against

~~Y against X~~

일반적으로, 두 변수(變數) 사이의 관계를 나타내는 경우에는 이 단어가 쓰이지 않는다. 이때, 다음 표현이 쓰인다.

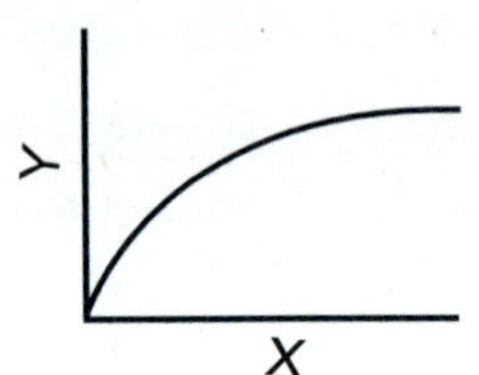

The graph shows...
We measured...

- Y **versus** X.
- **how** Y **varies with** X.
- **how** Y **changes with** X.
- **how** Y **depends on** X.
- Y **as a function of** X.
- **the dependence of** Y **on** X.

Figure 3 is a graph of Y **versus** X.

> Exception
> In this graph, Y **is plotted against** X.
> We **plotted** Y **against** X.

[Against]를 [stable], [robust], [flexible] 및 [difference]등과 함께 쓰지 않는다.

× *One drawback is the lack of flexibility against coding format.*
○ One drawback is the lack of **flexibility with regard to** coding format.

× *This state is robust against fluctuations in the background charge.*
○ This state is **robust with respect to** fluctuations in the background charge.

× *Feedback control provides good stability against external disturbances.*
○ Feedback control provides good **stability with regard to** external disturbances.

× *The strong confinement is due to the large refractive-index difference against air.*
○ The strong confinement is due to the large refractive-index **difference with respect to** air.

~~tolerance against~~  tolerance to

○ This device exhibits good **tolerance to** thermal noise.

A Capitals Z

1. [Section]과 [chapter] 뒤에 수치(數値)가 있는 경우, 이들 단어의 두문자(頭文字)로 할 것.

As mentioned in **S**ection 2, the main problem ...
... (see **C**hapter 5).

2. 절(節)의 첫 두문자(頭文字)를 대문자로 할 것.

1. **I**ntroduction
References

3. 화학물질 및 원소의 이름을 풀네임로 쓰는 경우, 두문자(頭文字)는 대문자로 하지 말 것.

Annealing was carried out in a **n**itrogen (N_2) ambient.
The n-type dopant was **s**ilane (SiH_4) and the p-type was diethylzinc (DEZn).

4. 단지 약어(略語) 및 기호가 대문자로 쓰여 있다고 해서 그것의 두문자(頭文字)도 대문자로 할 필요는 없다.

× *Solid-Oxide Fuel Cells (SOFCs) are attracting a great deal of attention ...*
○ Solid-**o**xide fuel **c**ells (SOFCs) are attracting a great deal of attention ...

× *... a novel Voltage-Controlled Oscillator (VCO) ...*
○ ... a novel **v**oltage-controlled oscillator (VCO) ...

- Dash -

NOTE 대시는 기술영어에선 별로 쓰지 않는다. 그 기능은 콤마와 괄호에 의해 실현될 수 있다. 대시 전후(前後)에는 스페이스를 넣지 않는 것에 주의하라.

1. 리스트

The complete circuit—quadrature frequency divider, dual interpolators at *f*/2, and an XOR frequency doubler—performs the function of a phase shifter running at the full frequency of the system clock.

2. 코멘트

One or both of the above effects can be expected in many—if not most—relevant experimental situations.

Behavioral VHDL models of burst-mode state machines can be very lengthy—over 1,600 lines of VHDL code.

/ Slash /

슬래시에 있어서의 문제는, 의미가 엄밀히 정의되어 있지 않은 것이다. 슬래시는 [or]를 의미하지만, 예를 들면 [washer/dryer]나 [clock/radio]처럼 두 물체가 결합하여 만들어진 물건이던가, 또는 두 기능을 가진 경우, 슬래시는 [and]를 의미한다. 슬래시의 의미는 엄밀히 정해져 있지 않으므로, **표준적인 전문용어 이외에는 쓰지 않는 편이 좋다**.

예를 들면, 다음 예를 생각해 보자.

× *The circuits might undergo <u>physical/chemical</u> degradation.*

이 문장에서 여러 가지 해석이 있다.

A. The circuits might undergo **either physical degradation or chemical degradation, but not both**.

B. The circuits might undergo **physical degradation or chemical degradation or both**.

C. The circuits might undergo **both physical and chemical degradation**.

이 정도의 부정확한 기술논문(技術論文)은 적절치 않다. [or]라는 의미라면, [or]라는 단어 자체를 쓰는 쪽이 좋고, [and]라는 의미라면 [and]라는 단어 자체를 쓰는 쪽이 좋다. 그래서 양쪽을 의미하는 것이라면, [and/or]를 써야 한다.

○ The circuits might undergo **physical and/or chemical degradation**.

전문 용어(用語)에서는 슬래시는 여러 가지 의미가 있다.

AND
I/O circuits (input **and** output circuits)
fingerprint sensor/identifier LSI (fingerprint sensor-**and**-identifier LSI)
the read/write functions of a RAM (read **and** write functions)

TO
A/D converter (analog-**to**-digital converter)
O/E conversion (optical-**to**-electrical conversion)

STRUCTURE
Si/SiO_2 interface (the interface between Si/SiO)
CMOS/SOI circuit (CMOS circuit made on an SOI wafer)

RATIO
ON/OFF ratio (ratio of voltage of ON signal to that of OFF signal)
S/N ratio (signal-to-noise ratio) (Also, SNR.)

WITH & WITHOUT
도표에서는, 단어 전체를 쓸 여유가 없는 경우, [with] 를 [w/], 그리고 [without]를 [w/o]로 쓰는 일도 있다.
w/ bias w/o bias

TYPICAL MISTAKES

× ... *the charge / discharge efficiency of a Ni/MH cell.*

NOTE 문장 중에서, 슬래시가 두 단어 사이에 쓰이고 있는 경우, 슬래시 전후에는 스페이스를 넣지 말 것.

○ ... the **charge/discharge** efficiency of a Ni/MH cell.

× ... *multilayers formed by ion-beam/helicon sputtering.*

○ .. multilayers formed by **ion-beam or helicon** sputtering.

× ... *receiver configurations for analog/digital optical transmission systems.*

○ ... receiver configurations for **analog and digital** optical transmission systems.

× ... *good accessibility to data/program resources ...*

○ ... good accessibility to **data and program** resources...

Prepositions 8

다음 빈칸을 메꾸어라. 필요없다면 X로 메꾸어라.

REVIEW

a. X is the same _________ Y.
b. X is effective _________ improving ...
c. There is no information _________ Y.
d. X has an effect _________ Y.
e. X brings _________ Y. [=cause]
f. X is _________ the order _________ 10^6.
g. X leads _________ Y.
h. X compensates _________ Y.
I. X is called _________ Y.
j. X takes Y _________ consideration.

CHECK YOUR KNOWLEDGE

1. In Fig. 1, the diagram _________ the top is ...
2. In Fig. 2, the diagram _________ the bottom is ...
3. In Fig. 3, the diagram _________ the left is ...
4. In Fig. 4, the diagram _________ the right is ...
5. In Fig. 5, the diagram _________ the middle/center is ...
6. The key _________ X is ...
7. There is a difference _________ X and Y.
8. There is a difference _________ length _________ X and Y.
9. The best approach _________ X...

References

1) Nicholas J. Higham: *Handbook of Writing for the Mathematical Sciences*, Society for Industrial and Applied Mathematics (1998)

2) John A. Borgan: *Clear Technical Writing*. McGraw-Hill (1973)

3) *Shogakukan Progressive English-Japanese Dictionary*, 2nd ed., Shogakukan (1987)

4) William C. Paxson: *The New American Guide To Punctuation*, Penguin (1986)

5) *American Heritage Dictionary*, 2nd college ed., Houghton Mifflin (1982)

6) L. G. Alexander: *Longman English Grammar*, Longman (1988)

Answers

Section 1

realize

1. fabricate/make/construct
2. provide/obtain/yield
3. implement/perform/carry out
4. build/construct/make/fabricate
5. fabricate/make
6. perform/carry out
7. perform/carry out/provide
8. yield/provide/obtain
9. construct/build/make
10. fabricate/make
11. achieve/provide
12. perform/carry out
13. fabricate/make
14. obtain/yield/provide
15. perform/carry out

evaluate vs. estimate

PART A

1. evaluate
2. estimate
3. estimate
4. estimate
5. evaluate

   NOTE: If performance has previously been defined to be a particular variable such as speed, then it is possible to estimate the performance.
6. evaluate
7. evaluate
8. estimate
9. estimate
10. evaluate

    NOTE: If efficiency refers to a specific characteristic or property, such as absorption efficiency or conversion efficiency, then it is possible to estimate the efficiency.
11. *estimate*

PART B

1. determined/estimated
2. identified/determined
3. observed/examined/investigated
4. examine/investigate/determine
5. examined/investigated/determined
6. observe/examine/investigate
7. measured/examined/investigated

propose

1. devised/created/developed
2. the/a fabricated/our new
3. devised/developed/created
4. describes/reports on
5. developed/devised
6. reported/developed/devised

Dynamic Verbs 1

1. Hot electrons **were injected into** the transistors.
2. Figure 3 **illustrates** the

experimental setup.

3. ...the wavelength is converted from λ_{in} to λ_{out}.
4. The polymer layer **was removed** by ...
5. Growth **was interrupted** ...
6. ... the electrical interface **limits** the bandwidth

Prepositions 1

1. ×	4. as	7. ×	10. on
2. ×	5. to	8. ×	
3. to	6. of	9. ×	

Section 2

in case of fire

1. The values are 8.4 mW **for Device** A and 11.2 mW **for Device B**.
2. This phenomenon appears only **when the input power is greater than a certain value**.
3. This figure shows pulse patterns **for an output voltage of 200 mV**.
4. **When the numerical aperture is low**, V_b has no effect.
5. These figures show the performance **for 156-Mbit/s signals**.
6. The resistivity increased monotonically with annealing time **when the zirconium layer was 200 nm thick**.
7. **When the total thickness is greater than 1μm**, the coupling efficiency is much larger.
8. Chemical polishing reduces the threshold voltage **for long-channel devices**.
9. **When a defect is completely within the silicon**, it does not give rise to a gate oxide defect.
10. **For thin barriers**, IRIT increases with barrier thickness.

Combining Nouns

1. **the length of** the Si-Si bond
2. **the change in** the critical dimension
3. **calculation of** the intensity and pattern profiles
   calculation of the intensity profile and the pattern profile
4. **the scanning frequency of** the mirror
5. **the thickness of** the GaAs buffer layer
6. **the replication of** sub-100-nm patterns
7. **the etching of** small contact holes
8. at **coding rates of** less than 10 Mbit/s
9. **a method of** controlling **the amount of** surface acid

contain vs. include

1. contains

2. including
3. included
4. contains/includes
5. included
6. contain
7. include
8. includes
9. contain/include
10. including
11. include
12. including
13. contain
14. contains
15. include
16. includes
17. includes

compared to vs. than

1. This method is **much more effective than** conventional ones.
2. the processing power is **much lower than** that of conventional machines.
3. The efficiency is **much smaller than** that of the other devices.
4. The current gains are **much higher than** this value.
5. The new circuit is **about 25% smaller than** a conventional one.
   The size of the new circuit is **about 25% smaller than** that of a conventional one.
6. The accuracy is **lower than** that of the simulation results.

Hyphen

1. a 15-minute presentation
2. a gate width of 5 μm
3. We made 3-micron-long devices.
4. We made 3-micron-long devices.
5. OK
6. OK
7. We made a device 3μm long.
8. OK
9. OK
10. high-temperature superconductors
11. a one-dimensional system
12. a high-oversampling frequency of 6 MHz
13. OK
14. a GaAs buffer layer 480 nm thick
15. a 0.5-μm-thick layer of resist
16. lattice-matched substrates
17. a low-voltage LSI
18. OK
19. at a low V_{th}

Dynamic Verbs 2

1. The calculations **take** these atoms into account.
2. Wire bonding **generates** mechanical stress.
3. A lens **focused** the optical signal on the device.
4. Our circuit technique **suppresses** the output jitter.
5. The feedback dramatically **improves** the characteristics.
6. The thin p+ layer **raises** the

conduction band.

7. This electrical excitation **generates** ballistic electrons in the diodes.
8. This model **includes** the gate-drain capacitance.
9. Using this circuit **reduces** the number of connections by 75%.

Prepositions 2

a.	to	1.	of	6.	with
b.	×	2.	on	7.	×
c.	×	3.	×	8.	on
d.	×	4.	to	9.	for
e.	as	5.	to	10.	of

Section 3

for -ing

1. OK
2. OK
3. **To measure**
4. ...**to control**
5. **To track**
6. ...**to reduce**
7. OK
8. ...**to verify**
9. ...**to improve**
10. OK
11. OK/ ...to examine ...
12. ...**to assess**
13. OK
14. OK

can, could

1. can demonstrate → demonstrates
2. OK/ can operate → operate
3. OK
4. can be estimated → was estimated
5. OK, but "prevents" is better.
6. OK. "prevents" is OK, too.
7. can be → are
8. OK
9. OK, but "blocks" is better.
10. can improve → improves
11. OK
12. can obtain → obtained

becomes vs. is

PART A

1. OK
2. As V_{DD} **becomes smaller**, ...
3. ..., Z **is** negligible.
4. OK

PART B

1. OK
2. ...the gain of one stage is G_a/n...
3. ..., Z **is** negligible.
4. ...it **is** necessary
5. OK

Unnecessary Repetition

1. ...observing **it**
2. **It** was removed...
3. ...**it** has no mask...
4. **It** can also be...

5. **It** minimizes areas...
6. **The results revealed that they are relaxed in two steps.**
7. **It** was fabricated...

Prepositions 3

a.	to	h.	on	5.	in
b.	on	i.	×	6.	of
c.	×	j.	of	7.	with
d.	with	1.	for	8.	from
e.	for	2.	to	9.	on, of
f.	on	3.	×	10.	to
g.	×	4.	on		

Section 4

respectively

1.	WRONG	7.	WRONG
2.	WRONG	8.	OK
3.	OK	9.	OK
4.	OK	10.	WRONG
5.	WRONG	11.	OK
6.	OK		

common vs. popular

1. common/popular
2. common
3. popular
4. common
5. popular
6. common/popular
7. common

recently

1. OK
2. These systems **are now being investigated** ...
3. Recently, the operating speed of CMOS LSIs **reached** about 4 GHz.
5. OK
6. A great deal of attention **is now being paid** to these defects.
7. X-ray lithography <u>was applied</u> to the fabrication of this circuit in 2005. (통상, [recently]는 특정한 시간과 함께 사용하지 않는다.
8. OK
9. **Nowadays**, portable equipment uses low-voltage LSIs.
10. This method **is now** widely used.
11. OK
12. OK
13. It is **now** becoming more important to reduce costs.

Adjective Formation (-ed)

PART A

1. computer-aided design
2. boron-doped silicon
3. a laser-generated pulse

PART B

1. shoes that are made by hand
2. components that are based on semiconductors
3. a technique that is oriented toward speed

Adjective Formation (-ing)

PART A

1. a wafer-holding mechanism
2. zirconium-containing copper
3. industry-leading performance

PART B

1. fiber that reduces dispersion
2. techniques that reduce noise
3. equipment that bonds wires

Adj. Formation: Practice

1. It is a water-rinsed resist.
2. It is a packed-switching network.
3. It is pan-fried rice.
4. She is a college-educated woman.
5. It is a current-blocking structure.
6. It is letter-sorting equipment.
7. It is a low-temperature-grown device.
8. They are user-specified parameters.
9. It is a rate-limiting factor.

Comma 1

1. Also, both designs use amplifiers.
2. As this model suggests, holes can drift through the channel.
3. At 50 kV, about half the electrons pass through the silicon
4. This provides an extra gate drive, V_{kink}, to the transistor.
5. Using multipass writing, we have demonstrated 36-nm image placement.
6. Table 2 compares length, area, and execution times for each case.
7. When sufficient current is injected, as the clock rises, the voltage follows the clock.
8. Finally, the spectra range in amplitude from 10^{-5} to as much as 10^{-2}.
9. Consider, as an example, an ASIMD chip with a SynchLink interface.
10. The top curve shows the reflectance, R, measured at room temperature.

Unnecessary Words 1

1. The <u>shielding</u> provided by...
2. ...we employ <u>regrowth</u>.
3. OK
4. Anisotropic Si <u>etching</u> is one of the most important technologies for bulk <u>micromachining</u>.
5. The <u>collimation</u> is caused ...
6. OK
7. This structure is essential for achieving <u>a low threshold current and a high output power</u>.
8. ...<u>offset-canceling</u> is ...
9. We use two special techniques for the fabrication: image <u>reversal</u> and pattern-dependent <u>oxidation</u>.
10. ...the suppression of current <u>blocking</u>.
11. OK *[NOTE: A bridge is not a*

kind of technique.]

12. The p+ regions are formed by Zn diffusion during alloying.
13. This device employs a Coulomb blockade to manipulate...
14. OK

Prepositions 4

a.	for	i.	on, of	6.	in
b.	to	j.	×	7.	to
c.	×			8.	on, about
d.	for	1.	with		
e.	on	2.	to	9.	between
f.	×	3.	to	10.	×
g.	of	4.	into		
h.	of	5.	to		

Section 5

has been used vs. is used

1. OK
2. A lot of multimode fiber **is being** used for LANs in office buildings.
3. Three main methods **are used** to grow crystals of organic materials.
4. OK
5. OK
6. GaAsFETs **are widely used** in circuits operating at microwave frequencies.
7. OK
8. The amplifier we developed **is being used** in the transmitter and receiver of a 120-GHz-band wireless system.
9. OK
10. Conventionally, lead-acid batteries **are used** for backup power supplies.

by vs. with

1.	with	5.	with	9.	by, by
2.	with	6.	with	10.	with
3.	by	7.	with	11.	with
4.	by	8.	by		

Broken Connection

1. **a method of estimating/an estimation method for** the current
2. ...results **similar to** those ...
3. ...signals **transmitted over** our new microstrip line
4. a new **technique for trimming** planar lightwave circuits.
5. Data **stored in a 1-V SRAM** is destroyed at a voltage of 1.8 V.
6. **a method of designing / a design method** for DC electric-power-supply networks
7. **a technique for integrating / an integration technique for**
8. a performance **similar to** that ...
9. The bias voltage **applied to** the device ...

multi-

1. multichannel receiver
2. multichip module
3. multifunction circuit
4. multilayer(ed) structure
5. multiprocessor system

Comma 2

1. On the other hand, if X is low, Y will be low after the clock goes high.
2. These points are illustrated in Fig. 1, which compares three types of spectra for a typical semiconductor, GaAs.
3. As shown in Fig. 2, the sample is extrinsically modulated by a source at some frequency, f.
4. High voltage reduces scattering, resulting in better resolution, straighter side walls, and reduced proximity effects.
5. With image placement targets as low as 35nm, all contributions must be minimized, including those from the e-beam system and process-induced distortion.
6. However, if these constraints are present, problems arise if one attempts to simplify the timing graph.
7. In the transmission mode, the spectrum is the relative change in transmittance, ΔT/T.
8. When the clock input is low, transistors P3 and P4 act as resistive loads for the first stage, which acts as a linear amplifier for small input swings and as a swing-limiter for large input swings.
9. Common digital layout procedures, such as symbolic layout and layout compaction, destroy the symmetry of critical analog layouts, impacting performance.
10. All cases used 0.75-μm-thick PMMA resist, with the results being an average for isolated lines, isolated spaces, and equal-line/space arrays.
11. To maintain quasi-neutrality, the electron concentration must be increased, resulting in reduced source resistance.
12. In this model, holes drift into the low-field source-gate region, where they diffuse and recombine.

Unnecessary Words 2

PART A

1. The first test **clarified** the degradation modes.
2. Optical fibers **transport** light to and from the probe.
3. A teflon lens **focused** the signal on the detector.

4. This terraced structure **improves** the heat dissipation of the chip.
5. An electro-optic probe **detected** reflected and transmitted signals.
6. The tungsten **reduces** the resistance of the source, drain, and gate.

PART B

1. Withe optical fiber, there is a small power penalty.
2. The spectrum is similar down to an input power of −5 dBm.
3. Without an RF bias, a definite peak appears at 1.4 Å. (..., there is a definite peak at 1.4 Å.)
4. There is no peak shift either with or without an RF bias.
5. The edge of the pattern is distorted, and the side wall is not vertical.
6. The eye openings are clear and well defined.

Prepositions 5

a.	of	h.	in	4.	of
b.	to	I.	with	5.	in
c.	to	j.	to	6.	on, about
d.	with			7.	to
e.	between	1.	with	8.	of
f.	to	2.	to	9.	in
g.	into	3.	to	10.	in, by

Section 6

most vs. most of

1. **Most of** the diodes we fabricated...
2. OK
3. OK
4. OK
5. ...**most** fingerprints.
6. **Most of the** carbon dioxide in the chamber...
7. OK
8. **Most of the** beryllium atoms...

issue

1.	problem	7.	problem
2.	issue	8.	issue
3.	issue	9.	issue
4.	problem	10.	problem
5.	problem	11.	issue
6.	issue		

Semicolon

1. The open circles are for the pile-up model; and as you can see, the agreement is excellent.
2. This figure illustrates a number of key characteristics of the kink: The kink in I_D occurs approximately at a constant V_{DG} of 1.2 V; the size of the kink appears to increase with increasing V_{GS}; and the onset of the kink coincides with the appearance of I_{SG} and with a

prominent rise in E_G, presumably due to hole collection by the gate.

3. Below the line, diffusion is dominant; and above, drift is dominant.
4. Unlike digital LSIs, most of the area of MMICs is occupied by passive elements, such as transmission lines, inductors, and capacitors; and reducing their size is the best way to miniaturize MMICs.
5. Circuit extraction is an important step in VLSI circuit design verification; it provides the link between the physical design and its verification phases.
6. As you can see, when the phase is 160°, the best-focus position does not shift at all; and the depth of focus is as wide as that without spherical aberration.
7. The data timing is ideally centered at zero and tracks the data bit rate; it is ideally ±0.75 ns at a data bit rate of 1.5 ns, and ±1.5 ns at a data bit rate of 3.0 ns.

Prepositions 6

a.	to	h.	to	5.	into
b.	to	i.	to	6.	with
c.	×	j.	×	7.	for
d.	to	1.	from	8.	with
e.	of	2.	in	9.	into
f.	with	3.	of	10.	on
g.	for	4.	into		

Section 7

Bad Passives

1. The variation in lasing frequency among the devices **originates** in the fabrication process.
2. A 30-nm-thick layer of SiO_2 **remained** on top.
3. The GaAs layer **may disappear** during overetching if the microwave power is too high.
4. Limit-cycle oscillations **occur**.
5. It is impossible to avoid the bandwidth limitation **originating** from the carrier response of the semiconductor.
6. A high power density enables nonlinear optical effects **to occur**.
7. The data stored in the selected memory cells **appear** on the bit lines.
8. This high value suggests that hydrogen passivation still **remains**.

know vs. find out

1.	find out	7.	know
2.	know	8.	find out
3.	find out	9.	know

4. find out/know 10. find out/know
5. find out
6. find out

maintain vs. remain

1. The output power **remains** constant.
2. When 1530 nm$\leq\lambda\leq$1570 nm, the extinction ratio **remains over 13 dB**.
3. The Ni and Ti contents **remained the same** during the ion-exchange process.
4. The optical quality of the output light **should remain the same**, even after thousands of circulations.
5. The energy profile around the edge **remains steep**.
6. The return loss **remained sufficiently high**.

difference

1. between
2. in, between
3. in, between, in
4. in, of
5. between
6. between
7. in, between
8. in, between
9. between
10. in
11. in, of, between

Prepositions 7

a. into	h. from	4. on
b. from	i. ×	5. on
c. with	j. on	6. in
d. of		7. in
e. of	1. to	8. in, with
f. with	2. to	9. in
g. ×	3. about	10. about

Section 8

whose

1. ...a signal **with** a wavelength **of** 1300 nm.
2. ...pulses **with** a width **of** less than 30 ps.
3. ...beam **with** a diameter **of** about 6 nm.
4. ...signals **with** frequencies **that** extend down to several kilohertz.
5. ...antenna **with** teeth **that** correspond to frequencies from 150GHz to 2.4 THz.
6. ...converter **with** capacitors **that** are fabricated on the chip.
7. ...access, **which** has a top speed of 622 Mbit/s,...
8. ...module, **which** is the same size as a standard LD module.
9. ...49 dB, **which** satisfies the specifications ...
10. ...signals, **for which** the DC level is not usually 0 V.
11. ...10-50 eV, **for which** the mean free paths are from one-half to a

few nanometers long, ...

12. ...transistor **for which** the electrical properties had been measured beforehand.

Prepositions 8

a. as
b. in
c. on, about
d. on
e. about
f. on, of
g. to
h. for
i. ×
j. into

1. at
2. at
3. on
4. on
5. in
6. to
7. between
8. in, between
9. to

Index

저자 약력

Richard Cowell(리처드 카우얼)
1970 스탠포드대학교 수학과 졸업
1980 인텍 저팬 (株) 근무

佘 錦華(Jin-Hwa She)
1993 동경공업대학원 이공학연구과
박사 후기 과정 수료
박사 (공학)
1993 동경공과대학 강사
2001 동경공과대학 조교수

역자 약력

이 재 호
성균관대 영문학과 명예교수
저서 「영한사전비판」(2005) 「문화의 오역」(2005) 외에
50여권의 번역서가 있음

과학기술 영작문의 기본
Mastering the Basics of Technical English

초판발행 2008년 8월 25일
재판발행 2011년 1월 10일

저자 Richard Cowell · 佘錦華
역자 이재호
펴낸이 홍정수
펴낸곳 탐구당
출판등록 1950. 11. 1 서울 제 03-00993호
주소 | 140-011 서울특별시 용산구 한강로1가 158
전화 | (02)3785-2211~5 | 팩스 (02)3785-2272
e-mail | tamgudang@tamgudang.co.kr
http://www.tamgudang.co.kr

ISBN 978-89-87314-30-3 13740
값 12,000원